LETTERS TO THE
THESSALONIANS

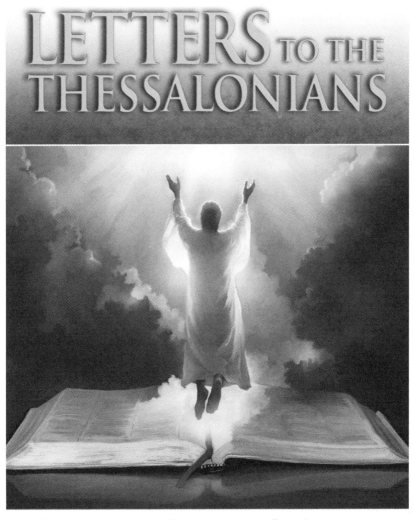

Jon Paulien

Pacific Press® Publishing Association
Nampa, Idaho
Oshawa, Ontario, Canada
www.pacificpress.com

Cover design and resources from Lars Justinen
Inside design by Aaron Troia

The author assumes full responsibility for the accuracy of all facts and quotations as cited in this book.

Additional copies of this book are available by calling toll-free 1-800-765-6955 or by visiting http://www.adventistbookcenter.com.

Library of Congress Cataloging-in-Publication Data:

Paulien, Jon, 1949-
    Letters to the Thessalonians / Jon Paulien.
        p. cm.
    ISBN 13: 978-0-8163-2626-6
    ISBN 10: 0-8163-2626-6 (pbk.)
    1. Bible. N.T. Thessalonians—Commentaries. I. Title.
    BS2725.53.P38 2012
    227'.8107—dc23
                                                                    2011048015

12 13 14 15 16 • 5 4 3 2 1

Dedication

This book is dedicated to a former teacher, Ivan Blazen,
and a former student, Richard Choi,
who have become colleagues and dear friends.
They have inspired me with a love for Paul
and a deep appreciation for his ministry of the Word.

Other books by Jon Paulien

Table of Contents

Outline of the Thessalonian Letters

I. First Thessalonians
    A. Chapter 1:1–5: Greetings and Thanksgiving
    B. Chapter 1:6–3:13: Grounds for Thanksgiving
        1. 1:6–10: Congregational Imitation
        2. 2:1–12: The Apostolic Example
        3. 2:13–16: The Judean Example
        4. 2:17–3:10: Paul's Desire to See Them
            a) 2:17–20: Previous Attempts to Visit Them
            b) 3:1–5: Timothy's Substitute Visit
            c) 3:6–10: The Result of Timothy's Visit
        5. 3:11–13: Transitional Benediction
    C. Chapter 4:1–5:22: Admonitions
        1. 4:1–8: The Marriage Ethic
        2. 4:9–12: Communal Ethics
        3. 4:13–18: The Dead in Christ
        4. 5:1–11: The Eschaton
        5. 5:12–22: Congregational Life
    D. Chapter 5:23–28: Benediction

II. Second Thessalonians
    A. Chapter 1: Greetings and Thanksgiving
        1. 1:1, 2: Epistolary Prescript
        2. 1:3–12: Thanksgiving
    B. Chapter 2:1–12: The Thessalonian Apocalypse
    C. Chapter 2:13–3:5: Perseverance Assured
    D. Chapter 3:6–15: Exhortations
        1. 3:6–10: Discipline the Disorderly
        2. 3:11–13: To the Disorderly
        3. 3:14, 15: Disfellowship the Disobedient
    E. Chapter 3:16–18: Benediction

The Gospel Comes to Thessalonica

A young pastor and the newest member of his church, a young woman who had been baptized the previous week, sat together by a lake. "I need to be baptized again," she said matter-of-factly.

"Why?" the pastor asked.

"There are things I didn't tell the senior pastor about my past."

Thus began an extended conversation about youthful indiscretions and the forgiveness available in Christ. Then, recalling his ministerial training, the pastor led the woman through the sinner's prayer. When he said, "Amen," the heavens opened and a huge downpour drenched them both. Eyes shining, the young woman said, "I'm being baptized again!" She interpreted the rain shower as God's confirmation that she was right with Him.

A living God

A gracious God often provides tokens like that rain to assure believers that they are right with Him. Our God is a God of love. He enjoys showering His beloved ones with little gifts just to say "I love you." Perhaps you've sent up a brief prayer when you've lost hope of finding a parking space in time to meet a critical appointment—and immediately found a space. Or you've become distraught, wondering where your boy is, and you've prayed for him in desperation—and then the phone rang and your boy told you that all is well. Millions of believers around the world have experiences just like this every day. God is real, and He loves to make His presence known to those who are open to Him.

Right now the skeptic in you is saying, "Wait a minute! Are you trying to tell me that God rearranged the weather of a whole region so a young woman would feel closer to Him? Are you saying that God manages the comings and goings in every parking lot around the world just in case one of His followers needs a spot at the last minute? What about all the real heartaches in this world that are met with silence?"

These objections have serious weight. Believers often don't realize how trivial their experience of God's presence may seem to others who have suffered deeply. To someone who is feeling God's absence—something Jesus Himself experienced when He was on the cross (see Matthew 27:46 and parallels)—our glib stories of His working in our everyday lives can hurt like a knife thrust to the heart. It can seem to them that God answers only trivial prayers.

The story of Job makes it clear that there is no easy answer to the objections raised above, at least in this life. The tragedies Job experienced are unexplainable in earthly terms. They had to do with complexities in the larger universe that Job never understood. Even when God came down to talk with him in person (Job 38:1–41:34), He never mentioned the real reason for Job's suffering, the reason revealed to the reader of the story (Job 1:6–12; 2:1–7). Job's story tells us that we're in the midst of an ongoing cosmic conflict that affects all that we do and all that we experience. God's actions are sometimes limited by considerations raised by that conflict, considerations that we may never understand until eternity. Perhaps God's intervention in Job's situation would have upset the whole space-time continuum of the universe in a way even quantum physicists couldn't understand. God can't explain what we can't understand.

However, we do understand that divine intervention can change things in a way that later causes collateral damage. The good we want God to do in the present may cause harm of greater consequence in the future. There is an interesting biblical illustration of this: the story of Hezekiah as told in Isaiah 36–39.

Hezekiah was one of the most faithful kings to rule in Judah. When he was about to die, he pleaded with God for more time (Isaiah 38:1–3). God granted him fifteen more years (verse 5). However, those extra years brought two events that undid all the good he had done up to that time: the visit of the Babylonian envoys (Isaiah 39:1–8), and the birth of his son Manasseh, who became an extremely evil king (2 Kings 21:1–9). In the context of the cosmic conflict between God and Satan, major interventions in people's lives are very complicated. The ramifications are usually far beyond our understanding.

Having said this, I still want to argue that the young woman's placement of her confidence in God because of that rain shower wasn't a mistake. I can't explain the timing and the effort involved in God's actions, but I do believe that God would give a positive answer to our every prayer if pleasing us were the only consideration. If finding someone a parking space or timing a phone call wouldn't upset the space-time continuum of the universe, why wouldn't a loving God intervene? If a woman makes a full commitment to Jesus just as a rain cloud happens to be passing by and God knew His releasing a downpour would cause few problems in the cosmic conflict, why wouldn't He give her that assurance?

My point? The lower the ultimate stakes—the smaller the implications of any particular divine intervention for other matters—the more likely that a loving God can answer the prayers of His people as a token of His love. Having said that, those of us who have experienced this kind of intimacy with God need to be careful when and how we share such experiences with others. Our well-intentioned testimony can increase the pain of those who are hurting.

What does all of this have to do with the letters Paul wrote to the Thessalonian believers? These letters are grounded in Paul's confidence that God was working in his life and in the lives of the church members. Paul's prayers were making a difference in their lives (1 Thessalonians 1:2–5), and Paul experienced God's probing of his heart on a regular basis (1 Thessalonians 2:4). He believed that God could help arrange his travel plans (1 Thessalonians 3:9–11) and his missionary agenda (2 Thessalonians 3:1, 2). He saw God's hand in the daily spiritual growth of the church in Thessalonica (2 Thessalonians 1:11, 12; 2:13). He believed God intervened to protect His faithful ones from spiritual harm (2 Thessalonians 3:3). Even better, he saw all of these little interventions as anticipations of the great final intervention in which God will make everything right and finally explain all things (1 Thessalonians 4:15–17; 5:1–11; 2 Thessalonians 1:5–10; 2:1–12).

Can we trust the Bible?

Paul wanted the Thessalonians to have an even deeper experience with God than was theirs at the time he wrote to them. He wanted their confidence in God to be grounded in something more stable than the daily tokens of God's presence in their lives—he wanted the words of Scripture, which he had a part in producing (2 Peter 3:15, 16), to be the foundation of their lives. He said, "We also thank God constantly for this, that when you received the word of God, which you heard from us, you accepted it not as the word of men but as what it really is, the word of God, which is at work in you believers" (1 Thessalonians 2:13, ESV).

Paul believed that the Word of God is a solid foundation on which we can stand while trying to understand the seeming inconsistency of God's intervention on some occasions and not on others. While life experience with God is important, our confidence in Him will be even more solidly grounded when it is based on the clear teaching of His Word. The Bible provides truth that is universally relevant and that we can apply to every facet of our lives. In the fog of everyday circumstances, we can have a clearer picture regarding who we are and what our purpose in life is. To put it bluntly, the Bible claims to provide exactly what we need.

This raises an important question: Can we really trust that the Bible is the Word of God, given to guide our lives? In a scientific, skeptical, "whatever's right for you" kind of world, can we really have confidence in Scripture? Can we really believe what Paul wrote in the passage quoted above?

I believe we can. My belief rests on four reasons of the head and some additional reasons of the heart.

First, God uses prophecy to demonstrate that the Bible is more than merely the words of human beings. People can predict some events relatively accurately up to one, five, or ten years in advance, but laying out events hundreds and thousands of years in the future requires divine knowledge. The Bible contains such knowledge. The accuracy of prophecies such as Daniel 2 and Matthew 24 point to a God who reveals secrets that human beings cannot know on their own.

Paul, Silas, and Timothy began their ministry to the Thessalonians by demonstrating that Jesus fulfilled the prophecies about the Messiah. Acts 17:2, 3, tells us that when Paul arrived in Thessalonica, he reviewed the Messianic prophecies and then showed how Jesus fit their specifications.* As we discover a God who knows the future, we gain confidence that He can use His Word to read our hearts and guide us in the right path (see John 2:23–25; Hebrews 4:12, 13).

Second, I have confidence in the Bible because of how much physical evidence has been preserved. Most ancient books have come down to us in a few handwritten documents that often are in a fragmentary state or are merely translations of the originals. In contrast, our New Testament alone is based on around *fifty-eight hundred* different Greek manuscripts! While there are some interesting variations

---

* I detail Jesus' remarkable fulfillment of the Old Testament's Messianic prophecies in my book *Meet God Again for the First Time.*

in those manuscripts, more than 99 percent of the words in the New Testament text are supported by multiple pieces of evidence from different traditions and locations. The original words of the New Testament have not been manipulated or distorted. We can have confidence that the Bible we hold in our hands today is the Book God intended us to have.

Third, I have confidence in the Bible because of its account of the resurrection of Jesus. People doubt the resurrection of Jesus primarily because they're biased against the idea that anyone could actually be resurrected. But consider the empty tomb. It makes no sense apart from a resurrection. Why was the tomb empty? Why has the body of Jesus never been found? The enemies of Jesus had no motive for removing His body. And if they had His body in their control, why didn't they produce it when the disciples started proclaiming that He was resurrected? The enemies of Christian faith could have destroyed that faith in a moment if they'd had the body of Jesus!

Jesus' friends had no reason to remove His body either. They didn't believe He would allow Himself to die in the first place (Matthew 16:21–23; Mark 8:31–33), and they were very slow to believe in His resurrection when it actually did occur. There was a platoon of highly trained Roman soldiers guarding Jesus' tomb, so the theory that the disciples stole Jesus' body so they could claim He was resurrected makes no sense historically.

Think about it. The disciples went through all kinds of hardship and suffering—including torture and even death—as they traveled widely and preached about Jesus. If they had somehow stolen the body of Jesus, they would have known there was no resurrection, and they would have known they were suffering to perpetuate a hoax, a flat-out lie. Maybe one person would have been dumb enough to do that, but there were hundreds who claimed to have seen Jesus after His crucifixion (1 Corinthians 15:6). So purely in terms of the historical evidence, the best explanation for the empty tomb is that Jesus was, in fact, resurrected from the dead. And if the resurrection of Jesus really happened, no other miracle that the Bible tells us about is impossible or incredible.

Fourth, I trust the Bible because of archaeology. There was a time when people knew little about the ancient world. Whenever the Bible differed from what they thought was the case, they assumed it was the Bible that was in error. But more and more archaeological findings are verifying the historicity of the Bible. For example, the Bible places one of Jesus' miracles of healing at a "pool of Bethesda" in Jerusalem. For a long time, many scholars thought no such pool ever existed, that it's mention in a story in John's Gospel indicates that the story was fictional, which then called into question the truth of the entire Gospel. But archaeologists found that pool, strengthening our faith in the Bible. I could mention many more such examples, but space does not permit me to—so, let's move to reasons of the heart.

Ultimately, the Bible is self-authenticating. In other words, as we read the Bible, we become aware of the presence of God in the text. Millions of people over nearly two thousand years have testified to this awareness, and I have experienced it many times myself.

If you haven't experienced God's presence in the Bible, it may be because you're approaching the Bible as merely a book of history or as a book whose teachings are disputed. You may be standing in judgment of the Bible, seeking to determine what parts are true and what parts are not. Jesus Himself pours cold water over this approach (John 7:17). If the Bible is truly the Word of God, we ought to take it seriously; we shouldn't consider it trivial or take it lightly. The Spirit of God is bound up in this Word, and God will manifest Himself through it if we approach it with an open heart and mind.

One of the hardest things for human beings to obtain is a teachable spirit. We love to be right, and we bristle when anyone tries to correct us. But we must approach the Bible humbly because it was given to correct us. If we approach it with a teachable spirit, it will not only lead us away from the dead ends in our thinking, but it will also minister the presence of God into our hearts.

We gain confidence in Scripture the same way a couple gains confidence in each other: when we spend time with the Word, the God behind the Word will reach out to us. Over time, we will become increasingly aware of His presence.

Not only does the Bible bring God into our lives, it also meets our needs in other ways. It is almost as if God's Word can read our minds, discern our needs, and apply divine truth directly to our hearts. If you've never developed the kind of confidence in the Bible I've written about in this chapter, I invite you to taste and see for yourself. I believe that if you will read God's Word with an open heart, you will gradually come to experience what so many before you have experienced. God's Word will become real to you, and in the process, God Himself will become real to you too.

Approaching Thessalonica

The core principle behind Paul's method of conveying the gospel message to people was to meet them where they were (1 Corinthians 9:19–23). To the Jew, he became like a Jew. To the Gentile, he became like a Gentile. He became "all things to everyone" in the hope of winning as many as possible to the gospel. So in the pagan context of Athens, Paul didn't approach people with a biblical message. Instead, he used some free time to study the religious context of Athens (Acts 17:16, 22, 23), and when he had the opportunity to speak, he began where they were in their knowledge of God. He pointed them to Creation (verses 24–26) and the witness of nature concerning God's purpose for the human race (verses 27, 28), and instead of depending on the Bible's authority, he quoted two of their respected writers in support of his points. Only then did he try to stretch their minds to another level.

However, in Thessalonica, Paul began with a study of the Old Testament (verses 2, 3). He walked his Jewish audience through what their Scriptures said about the Messiah to come. Then he described what he and the other apostles had experienced concerning Jesus. His goal was to lead them to conclude that Jesus was the Messiah whom Scripture had foretold.

The prophecies about the Messiah in the Old Testament were not point-by-point predictions of the specifics of Jesus' life. Instead, God described the Messiah to come by way of analogies with the people and things the Israelites were familiar with. The Messiah would be a prophet like Moses (Deuteronomy 18), a king like David, a priest like Aaron, and a conqueror like Cyrus (Isaiah 45:1). The Old Testament Scriptures spoke of the One to come in terms of characters in Israel's past. Only in the light of Jesus' life, teaching, and ministry did the words of the Old Testament come alive, making it clear that He was the One foretold in the lives of the great ones of the past. What Paul taught about the Messiah must have run through the Jewish audience in Thessalonica like an electric shock. Suddenly, the teachings of the Bible they had thought obscure began to make sense.

Paul's teaching was spiritual, authentic, and relational. He used narrative to gain the people's interest and then drew out lessons that spoke to the present with power. In many ways, the same strategy works with the postmodern generation of today, which seeks truth through relationships and stories. Paul was truly a man for all seasons.

Conclusion

Do you remember the story with which I began this chapter? Here's the rest of it: I was the young pastor. I had been taught in college how to lead a person to Christ, but this was the first time I had ever actually done it. And when I did, an amazing thing happened— by helping the young woman find peace in Christ, I myself was converted!

I had gone through Adventist schools and knew all the doctrines. My parents had raised me in "the fear of the Lord" and had taught me the value of a disciplined life and the routines of Sabbath and family worship. I had read widely in the writings of Ellen G. White, I never missed church, and I always attended camp meetings and evangelistic programs. And I had received Bible studies from a sweet German saint and was baptized at the age of twelve. However, something was still missing.

In walking that young woman through the steps of salvation, I, too, walked through them. When the Holy Spirit touched her heart with the presence of God, He touched mine as well. As she heard the words I was speaking, I also heard them. So, along with her, I, too, found freedom in Christ that day.

That's one of the reasons we ought to witness for our faith. As we tell the stories of what God has done in the past, the power of those stories is reactivated in the present. As we work through the experiences of Paul and the Thessalonians in the rest of this book, it is my prayer that the same God who was present with them will become increasingly present in your life.

Whatever became of the young lady in the story? I jokingly tell people that she was my first Bible study, my first baptism, and my first wife! For some thirty-eight years now, we have been together, telling others the stories of what God has done for us. The strongest foundation for a marriage is built when the man and woman meet each other in the context of a relationship with God. When the spiritual foundation is solidly laid, the mental, emotional, and physical aspects of the relationship are far more likely to last for a lifetime. My wife and I have discovered what Paul and the Thessalonians discovered: God's ways are the best ways.

CHAPTER

Preserving Relationships

Relationships are delicate things. Jake and Allison were miserable together and miserable apart. Their repeated attempts to break up were foiled by overwhelming feelings of loss when they were apart. Reconnections brought joy for a day or two, and then the old flaws in the relationship would return. Jake would become irritated when Allison didn't do her hair the way he liked. Allison felt trapped when Jake tried to control whom she talked to and when she did things. Allison knew just what buttons to push to make Jake angry. He would become distracted when someone he considered prettier than Allison walked by. And on it went.

The summer between their junior and senior years of college was approaching. In the midst of spring finals, Jake and Allison took the time to discuss where their relationship was heading. They dearly wanted to remain friends, yet neither felt that at that point marriage was a good idea, so the relationship seemed to be heading toward a dead end. They managed to come up with a plan. They both would be staying on campus to work for the summer. Most of the other students would be gone, so the social pressures would be minimal. They agreed to stop seeing each other on a regular basis. They would be friendly when their paths crossed, but they wouldn't seek each other out. They wanted to find out whether they could remain friends without the deep ups and downs that had characterized their relationship. How would they react to seeing each other spend time with other "options"? They prayed and talked and prayed some more. Then it was time to move on. This seemed like the right course of action. They would just be friends from then on.

The summer started out fairly well. Jake worked forty hours a week in the college library, while Allison helped in the cafeteria and did some work with her parents off campus. And, as they had planned, they didn't seek each other out but did run into each other two or three times a week.

At first those encounters went fairly well. They enjoyed being friends without having the pressure of expectations for the future lurking in the background. But as the summer dragged on, Jake began to feel a deep longing for Allison welling up within him. He saw clearly the pettiness of his criticisms of her, and he saw how much he had hurt her by flirting with other girls. She loved the Lord and was kind to everyone, and she loved him and would have given everything she had to make him happy. Jake realized that he had done nothing but find fault about things she couldn't control, and he regretted deeply that his selfishness had come between them. He concluded that he and Allison could have a wonderful life together if only he would be a better person.

Jake's longing to be with Allison again burned within him, and he wondered what she was thinking. Was her heart aching for him as much as his was for her? Did she wish they were together again or had she moved on? Eventually, Jake felt that he couldn't go one minute longer without seeing her. But what if his seeking her out drove her further away? After all, they had agreed neither would contact the other with the object of getting together again. What should he do? Pick up the phone? Send an e-mail? What if he sent an e-mail or a text message and she responded with a rejection note? What if she didn't respond at all? But he *had* to do something! He *had* to know if she still loved him as much as he loved her.

So, he just had to send an e-mail. He titled it "Hello." His message said, "There are some things I need to talk about. If you are willing to meet with me, let's get together at the chapel at a quarter to ten tomorrow morning. You don't have to if you don't want to, but I'd like that."

Jake moved the cursor to the Send button, where it hovered for a while. Should he or shouldn't he click on it? At last, he did. Then he wondered if she would be online. Would she respond right away or think about it for a while? Would she respond at all?

Jake waited by the computer, his stomach churning. An hour passed. Then two. And then three. Still no response. He needed to get some sleep, so he went to bed but left his computer on so he would hear the ding of an incoming e-mail. Sleep didn't come anyway. Every time the computer dinged, he jumped out of bed and rushed over to look at the screen. E-mails were coming from everyone but her. As the hours of the night slipped by, hope began to dim. Sending the e-mail had been a big mistake. Not letting her go was a bigger mistake. If only he could call the e-mail back.

Then, at 6:07 A.M., the computer dinged again. Halfheartedly Jake staggered over to the computer. The e-mail was from Allison! The title was simply "Re: Hello." He hesitated, feeling almost sick to his stomach with both excitement and fear. Mustering his courage, he clicked on the e-mail. The message was short. "Yes. I'll meet you there. I agree we need to talk."

Jake almost exploded with excitement! She wanted to talk too! This time things would be different! This time he would be the kind of person she needed him to be. He didn't feel like eating. He didn't feel like doing anything but being with her. Nine forty-five seemed like forever away! Just to be sure he wouldn't miss her, he got to the chapel before 9:30 A.M. and positioned himself where he could see her walking toward the chapel from her parents' house.

Nine thirty. Nine thirty-five. Nine forty-one. There she was! Still a couple of hundred yards away, she was the picture he had held so often in his mind's eye. Every fiber of his being called him to run to her and sweep her up in his arms, but that wasn't the agreement. He intended to play by *all* the rules this time, so he waited nervously while she approached . . .

Longing for the Thessalonians

What does this story have to do with Paul's letters to the Thessalonians? They, too, reflect a relationship that is deep in feeling yet short on contact. Paul's first visit to Thessalonica lasted only a few weeks, yet something deep within his soul was stirred by the people he met there. We get a glimpse into Paul's emotional life in chapters 2 and 3 of 1 Thessalonians.

Paul hadn't wanted to leave them. The Greek words he used reveal that he felt forcibly "orphaned." But while there was a physical distance between them, there was no distance in Paul's heart. Like Jake's feelings for Allison, the bond Paul felt in his heart resulted in an intense longing for them and frantic efforts to return to Thessalonica (1 Thessalonians 2:17). He wanted to visit again because he missed them dearly. But in ways that Paul doesn't spell out for us, Satan prevented him from returning (verse 18).

Paul heard that the believers in Thessalonica were being rejected and persecuted on account of their faith. If only he could be there and encourage them to persevere! If they gave up the faith, all of his efforts for them would be in vain (1 Thessalonians 3:5). There is just a hint of Paul's humanness coming through here. He wanted his life to make a difference. To some degree, his sense of value or well-being was tied up in the success of his mission. If their faith was strong in spite of persecution, he just might be able to go on living (my paraphrase of verse 8)!

When Timothy returned from Thessalonica, Paul learned that not only was the Thessalonians' faith strong, but that they also had pleasant memories of him "all the time" (verse 6 in Greek) and that they longed to see him as much as he longed to see them. Why would Paul mention this unless he had cared about what they thought of him? Apparently, even apostles were tempted to worry about the opinions or feelings others held toward them. I find this encouraging when I am tempted to entertain similar thoughts. Even the great characters of the Bible struggled with relationships.

Stages of relationship

Relationships are delicate things. Many writers have addressed the stages of relationship, and there are many different schemas. I find the seven-step approach developed by two friends of mine, Bill Underwood and Ed Dickerson, to be the most helpful. If you keep these stages in mind, you can tell exactly where you are in each of your relationships. You also know exactly what must happen for the relationship to progress to the next stage.

For the relationship to develop, both parties must be willing to move to the next stage. If one party holds back, the relationship will stall at the level both parties are on. If one party tries to move a stage or two ahead of the other party, the relationship is likely to end—though the aggressive party may be able to save it at that lower level if he or she backs off.

1. Acquaintance. When people first meet, they exchange greetings and comment about the weather or whatever else they think they might have in common. They may take a quick stock of the other person's face, body type, and surface personality, weighing whether they want to enter into a deeper relationship or to leave things on the surface. At this stage, they consider the other person a "nodding acquaintance." This stage holds little or no risk.

We encounter many people in this category nearly every day. In most cases, we don't even know the other person's name. Most acquaintances never get much closer to us than the exchange of greetings. While circumstances may precipitate deeper relationships, the move to stage two usually happens because of the interest of one of the parties in going a little deeper.

2. Facts and reports. The second stage of friendship involves the exchange of facts and reports. At this stage, the parties reveal things that are of interest to them—that have some importance in their lives. To put it another way, they reveal things that are personal but that are not private. Relationships at this stage pose a small but real risk. The parties are testing the water of the relationship with ideas that are central to who they are, and if one party isn't interested in what the other party shares, the party doing the sharing can feel hurt. If, on the other hand, the two parties find they have interests in common and they share their perspectives, the relationship can move past stage one into the exchange of useful information.

3. Opinions and judgments. Parties who want to go deeper in their relationship don't just talk about the weather. They move on to sharing some of their opinions and judgments. They throw out an opinion about politics or the latest world events, checking to see if it's safe to go deeper with the other party. If they find the other party to be a kindred spirit on a lot of issues, the relationship is likely to progress even further. At this stage, the level of risk is considerably higher. To be rejected because of the opinions one holds is more painful than to be rejected for mistaking a fact or for greeting someone in a way thought to be inappropriate. People's opinions and judgments lie closer to the core of their being.

4. Feelings. Friends reach stage four when they are willing to share feelings as well as facts and opinions. Human beings are very vulnerable at this stage. They can find it quite devastating to share how they feel and then to be rejected. Consequently, people often move into this stage quite gingerly. As the relationship deepens, people become willing to share what makes them happy and what makes them sad. They are willing to share what makes them angry or afraid. To share one's emotions is to become vulnerable to another. When that vulnerability is respected and affirmed by both parties, the relationship can go deeper yet.

There are many cultures in which people commonly express feelings of anger but suppress other feelings, such as fear, happiness, or sadness. When someone is willing to share his or her true feelings with you, he or she is trusting you a great deal. Paul uses a lot of feeling language to describe his relationship with the Thessalonians.

5. Failures and mistakes. Stage five is the make-or-break point in many relationships. People whose relationship has reached this stage are willing to share not only their opinions and judgments, their joys and fears, but they are also willing to admit their failures and mistakes. Most people must have a great deal of trust in another person before they're willing to say, "I was wrong."

When one party confronts the other about some mistake or offense and the guilty party offers excuses or makes accusations rather than admit the fault, the guilty party is avoiding the move to this level of relationship. If one party becomes defensive when the other party asks leading questions, it is probably time for the second party to back off to the previous level of relationship until trust has grown. In stage five, the two parties become truly vulnerable with each other.

6. Accountability. At stage six, the level of trust has become so high that the parties involved are willing to allow each other to point out their faults and to hold them accountable in their personal lives. They give their friends permission to confront them whenever their behavior is damaging to themselves, to others, or to their relationship. They allow the other party to have some control over their lives.

A common problem in marriage occurs when one spouse confronts the other as if they were both at stage six, but the other partner's defensiveness makes it clear that he or she hasn't reached this level yet. A similar problem arises in one-on-one evangelistic outreach: one party feels a need to confront other people about their behaviors or beliefs, but if the party hasn't welcomed similar intimacy from the others, the relationship is one sided and his or her approach is likely to be rejected. When the other party is defensive, the first party needs to back off to an earlier stage and pray for the

Holy Spirit's softening influence on his or her own heart as well as on the other person's heart.

7. Total intimacy. Stage seven is the stage of total intimacy, the stage where the two parties keep no secrets from each other. At this stage, everything is open and transparent to the other person. Few people in this life reach this stage, although it is a worthy goal for deep friendships and for marriage. A relationship of this depth is not easily broken.

While Paul had lived among the Thessalonians for only about a month, his relationship with them went very deep, certainly to the point where he could share some of his deepest feelings with them. And Paul could hardly wait to continue deepening the relationship. He eagerly awaited the Second Coming, when people will be able to deepen their relationships without the hindrance posed by distance or dysfunction.

Conclusion

Paul's longing for the Thessalonians came to a positive conclusion. They missed him just as much as he missed them. It was only a matter of time till he would find a way to return to Thessalonica, and then their relationship, so newly entered into, could flourish and grow as they had face-to-face contact again. In the meantime, however, letters and mutual friends would keep the fires burning, much as e-mails, text messages, and Skype aid long-distance relationships today.

What about Jake and Allison? How did their 9:45 encounter turn out?

Jake was careful not to touch Allison when he greeted her, while still being as friendly and welcoming as he could be. Allison's body language was hard to read; she seemed reserved in a way that he couldn't quite figure out.

Jake plunged into how much he missed Allison and how much he wanted them to be together again. He shared his determination to be a better person and to make it work this time, all the while looking into her eyes and longing for some indication of her heart's response.

When she finally spoke, it was through tears that were just barely suppressed. "I have the solution to the difficulties in our relationship," she said. "We can't stand being together, and we can't stand being apart. Every time we come together, we promise that things will be different, but they never are. So here's my solution: I've decided to go back home [a country three thousand miles away]. That way we can each start over again."

"No way," Jake responded. "I'll miss you too much. I'll go crazy without you. Let's keep trying. I'm sure we can work it out."

"I don't think so," Allison said. "We've been trying for two years. It's just not working out."

"Aw, come on," Jake pleaded. "Just one more chance. If you go away, my life will be ruined."

"No, it won't," Allison replied. "It'll be better for you if I go away."

But Jake wasn't convinced.

A week later, they stood in silence at the entrance to the airport security area. There was nothing left to say. All the talking and all the crying they had done had left them empty and exhausted. Allison handed the security agent her boarding pass and ID and then went through the gate into the security zone. As Jake watched her walk out of sight, her words kept ringing in his ears: *"It'll be better for you if I go away."*

He never saw her again.

Relationships on this earth are delicate things. They are forged in much uncertainty and challenged by temperament, distance, emotions, expectations, and much more. In Paul's case, the outcome was positive in the long run, although his relationship with the Thessalonians remained a long-distance one on the whole.

Paul's burning desire to be with the Thessalonians fueled his longing for the second coming of Jesus (1 Thessalonians 2:19, 20). Only that event would enable him to be with them as much as he desired. Only then could they go as deep into intimacy as they wished.

On this earth, at this time, all relationships eventually come to an end. But then we will know even as we are known (see 1 Corinthians 13:12). This is truly a blessed hope.

CHAPTER

Meeting People
Where They Are

The more familiar you are with the Bible, the clearer it becomes that God gave every part of it in the time, place, language, and culture of specific human beings. Paul, with his "PhD," expresses God's revelation in a different way than does Peter, the fisherman. John writes in simple, clear, almost childlike Greek, while the author of Hebrews writes in complex, literary Greek. In Matthew, you have someone who understands the Jewish mind and seeks to meet it, while Mark, on the other hand, reaches out to the Gentile mind.

The Greek language of the New Testament is quite different from the classical Greek of Plato and Aristotle. In the nineteenth century, many scholars thought New Testament Greek was some sort of "heavenly language," different from any other form of ancient Greek. Then, in 1896, two British archaeologists began excavating the ancient town of Oxyrhynchus in Egypt. They stumbled upon a massive garbage dump, with numerous piles as much as thirty feet high, composed of the rubbish of several centuries around the time of Christ and the apostles. The archaeologists also found everyday documents in the ruins of houses, and still others were buried in graves, some having been used to make decorations on the wrappings of mummies, both human and animal. In the dry climate of Egypt very little decomposition had taken place, so the ancient "trash" contained a treasure trove of well-preserved documents from everyday life in New Testament times—personal letters, wills, accounts, bills and receipts, and agreements regarding divorce, marriage, adoptions, and the sale of land.

When the scholars studied these everyday documents of the ancient Mediterranean world, they made a shocking discovery: The language in which they were written wasn't the scholarly Greek of Plato and Aristotle, nor was it the public Greek of law and government. Rather, it was the language that the writers of the New Testament had used! In other words, the New Testament wasn't written in a heavenly language nor in the cultured language of the traditional elite. Instead, it was written in the everyday language of everyday people. *In the language of the New Testament we see God going out of His way to meet people where they were!*

An example from Daniel

One might argue that the New Testament was written in everyday language because the people who wrote it were common folk, not intellectuals or members of the upper class, and they were simply using the language they knew—so God had nothing to do with it. But the evidence we find in the Bible shows otherwise. For instance, it's apparent that God adjusted the content of the visions in the book of Daniel to communicate His message as effectively as possible. The text makes this apparent.

Daniel 2 and Daniel 7 present the same basic message to two different men—two different "prophets," if you will. God gave each man a vision of four consecutive kingdoms that were followed by a divided kingdom, which, in turn, was followed by the kingdom of God (see Daniel 2:28–45; cf. 7:1–28). The message of each vision was that God is in control of the affairs of human history. He is the One who sets up kings and removes them, and His "son of man"

(Daniel 7:13, NIV) was to have dominion over the kingdoms of this world (Daniel 2:21; 7:13, 14, 27). So the two messages had virtually the same content.

To communicate His message about the future to the pagan King Nebuchadnezzar, God used the image of an idol, something Nebuchadnezzar could easily understand (Daniel 2:29–36). That the "image" of Daniel 2 was an idol is clear from Daniel 3. Nebuchadnezzar knew exactly what to do with that image—set it up to be worshiped! To Nebuchadnezzar, the great nations of the world were bright, shining examples of the gods they worshiped. God met him where he was.

To the Hebrew prophet Daniel, on the other hand, God portrayed the future in terms of the Creation story (Daniel 7:2–14; cf. Genesis 1; 2). The vision begins with a stormy sea upon which a wind is blowing (Daniel 7:2; cf. Genesis 1:2). Then animals appear (Daniel 7:3–6; Genesis 2:19, 20). And finally, there is a "son of man" who is given dominion over the animals (Daniel 7:13, 14; Genesis 1:26, 28). Daniel's vision is a powerful recollection of the Adam story in the Creation narrative. The message given in these images and references was something like this: just as Adam had dominion over the animals at Creation, God's "son of man," when He comes, will have dominion over the nations that were hurting Daniel's people. In other words, God is still in control of history, even when things look completely out of control. These two visions show that God meets people where they are. He certainly met Daniel and Nebuchadnezzar where they were.

The ultimate example of the principle that God meets people where they are is Jesus Himself. When God chose to reveal Himself in person, He didn't come as "Jesus Christ Superstar." Instead, He became a first-century Jew who lived in Palestine and who talked in terms appropriate to the local language and culture. He got dirty, hungry, and tired. At times, He even became frustrated, angry, and sad (see, e.g., Mark 3:4, 5; 10:13, 14). God didn't choose to send us a superstar; He sent us Someone just like ourselves. This principle is clearly articulated in *Selected Messages*:

The writers of the Bible had to express their ideas in human language. It was written by human men. These men were inspired of the Holy Spirit. . . .

The Scriptures were given to men, not in a continuous chain of unbroken utterances, but piece by piece through successive generations, as God in His providence saw *a fitting opportunity* to impress man at sundry times and divers places. . . .

The Bible is written by inspired men, but it is not God's mode of thought and expression. It is that of humanity. God, as a writer, is not represented. . . .

. . . The Bible, perfect as it is in its simplicity, does not answer to the great ideas of God; for infinite ideas cannot be perfectly embodied in finite vehicles of thought.[1]

It is this incarnation principle that motivated Paul in his missionary endeavors.

In 1 Corinthians 9:20–23, Paul tells us that it requires considerable sacrifice to reach out to people who differ from us.

To the Jews,
I become like a Jew
in order that I might win the Jews.
To those who are under the law,
I become like one under the law,
not being myself under the law,
in order that I might win those
who are under the law.
To those apart from law,
I become like one apart from law,
not being myself apart from the law of God
but rather under the law of Christ,
In order that I might gain those who are apart from law.

To the weak
I become weak
in order that I might win the weak.
I become all things to everybody
in order that by all possible means I might save some.

Ellen G. White noted, "Lessons must be given to humanity in the language of humanity."[2] People need to be addressed in a language with which they are familiar. The Adventist message is spreading like wildfire in places such as New Guinea, the Philippines, Kenya, and parts of the Caribbean because we usually express our message in terms that are exactly what people in those regions are looking for. In other places, the same message given in the same terms wouldn't touch the hearts of the population.

Paul applies the principle

Chapters 17 and 18 of the book of Acts picture Paul adjusting his message to meet several different kinds of situations. In Thessalonica, he started his work in a synagogue, beginning with a careful review of what the Old Testament taught regarding the Messiah (Acts 17:2, 3). When his audience understood the basic scriptural issues, he then shared the story of Jesus and the evidence that He met the criteria of Messiahship.

But when Paul went to Athens, he didn't march right up to the Areopagus* and give the philosophers there the same presentation he gave in the synagogue in Thessalonica. Instead, he walked around the city a bit, observing the people. Then he went to the marketplace of Athens and reasoned with whoever was willing (Acts 17:16–18). In the process, he provoked the curiosity of some Epicurean and Stoic philosophers, and they invited him to address them in the Areopagus, the traditional place for such discussions (verses 19, 20).

---

* Also known as Mars' Hill.

2—L. T. T.

When Paul addressed the intellectuals of Athens, he began with observations about their city and religions (verses 22, 23). Then he spoke of Creation, a topic that they both were interested in (verses 24–26). In contrast with his approach in the synagogue, he didn't argue his case from Scripture, but from writings that the intellectuals would have known. (Acts 17:27, 28 both echo and quote Greek writers.) It was almost as if Paul was searching for some kind of "Old Testament" in the background and thinking of the Athenians— some point of contact that would open their minds to the gospel. But while Paul was able to reach some people in Athens, he had to leave that city before he could raise up a major congregation there.

Paul must not have been satisfied with the results of his encounter with the philosophers of Athens, for when he went to Corinth, he decided to take a more direct approach to the Greek mind (1 Corinthians 1:18–2:2). He wasn't rejecting the idea of meeting people where they are, for he clearly promoted that approach in the same letter (1 Corinthians 9:19–23). What he demonstrated in Athens and Corinth is that meeting people where they are is not an exact science; it requires constant learning and adjustment. Paul didn't take the same approach in every city. He was very sensitive to changing times, cultures, and circumstances.

In Thessalonica, Paul did more than just speak to Jews on the basis of Scripture. He seems to have functioned something like street preachers do today. First-century Greco-Roman culture supported the proliferation of popular philosophers who sought to influence individuals and groups in public places. These philosophers were aware of the need to vary the message to meet different minds and of the importance of the integrity of both the teacher and his message. So there are numerous parallels between these popular teachers and Paul, who, like them, traveled from city to city and worked in the public places (Acts 17:17; 19:9, 10).

Of course, promoting a philosophy was an easier way to make a living than working with one's hands. That meant there were crowds of "traveling salesmen" trying to relieve people of their money. The ancients were well aware of the difference between authentic content and teaching motivated by the desire for money. In fact, Dio Chrysostom, a contemporary of Paul who was known to have visited Thessalonica, wrote the following words, which are strikingly reminiscent of 1 Thessalonians 2:3–6:

> To find a man who in plain terms and without guile speaks his mind with frankness, and neither for the sake of reputation or for gain . . . , but out of good will and concern for his fellow-men stands ready, if need be, to submit to ridicule and to the disorder and the uproar of the mob—to find such a man as that is not easy, but rather the good fortune of a very lucky city, so great is the dearth of noble, independent souls and such the abundance of toadies, mountebanks, and sophists.
>
> In my own case, for instance, I feel that I have chosen that role, not of my own volition, but by the will of some deity. For when divine providence is at work for men, the gods provide, not only good counsellors who need no urging, but also words that are appropriate and profitable to the listener.[3]

While there were some honest teachers, there was also a lot of cynicism about itinerant speakers. Paul sought to avoid some of that cynicism by generally refusing to accept money from his listeners and instead doing hard manual labor to support himself. This, along with his sufferings, demonstrated that he truly believed what he preached and that he wasn't in it for personal gain, as were so many others. Paul approached the Thessalonians, then, through a form familiar to them. And since that form of approach could be misunderstood, he adjusted it to avoid being confused with the kind of philosophers who exploited the people.

Tailoring the message

In addition to using a form of communication that would have been familiar to the average Greek-speaking Thessalonian, Paul seems to have tailored the message of the gospel to the Thessalonian situation. When the Romans took over the city some two hundred years before, the common people—especially the working classes—had suffered a great deal. The disruptions brought about by war and changing governments hit them harder than they did the wealthier people. And the working class suffered because of the exploitation that inevitably accompanies the occupation of one country by another. Roman officials siphoned off portions of the crops, minerals, and other local products and sent them to Rome to support the empire.

As the decades passed, the Thessalonians became increasingly frustrated, and their longing for a change in the situation grew. Political change seemed out of the question, so they looked to the spiritual realm for relief. A movement that scholars call the Cabirus cult arose among the pagans. This cult was grounded in a historical man named Cabirus, who spoke up for the disenfranchised and was murdered by his brothers. Followers of the cult regarded him as a martyred hero and buried him with symbols of royalty.

The lower classes believed that Cabirus's birth had been miraculous and that he exhibited miraculous powers while he was alive. They also believed that from time to time he quietly returned to life to help people and that one day he would return publicly to introduce a new age, bringing justice to the lower classes and restoring the city to its former independence and greatness. The Cabirus cult provided a hope for the oppressed, reminiscent of the biblical hope, something like a "pagan messianism."[4]

Things become even more interesting when we discover that the worship of Cabirus included baptism, confession, and blood sacrifices that commemorated his martyrdom. In words we have heard from Paul, the Thessalonians talked about "participation in his blood," through which they obtained relief from guilt. In the Cabirus cult, class distinctions were abolished and all its members were treated as equals.

There was one further dynamic. When the emperor cult arose in the time of Augustus (forty or fifty years before Paul's arrival in Thessalonica), the Romans proclaimed that Cabirus had come in the person of Caesar. In other words, the occupying authority co-opted the hope of the oppressed. As a result, the spiritual life of Thessalonica no longer provided relief for the working classes. The common people were left without a meaningful religion. The emperor cult also meant that if anyone resembling the real Cabirus were to arrive in the city, he would immediately be a threat to the ruling class of the city.

The Roman co-opting of the Cabirus cult left a spiritual vacuum in the hearts of the Thessalonians—one that only Christ could truly fill. The gospel provided both inner peace in the present and the promise of a reversal of the current economic and political realities at the Second Coming. At that time, the last would become first, and the exploiters would be exploited.

It still works today

In today's world, as in Paul's day, there are some people who can be reached directly through biblical preaching because they've heard such preaching since childhood and they respect the Bible's authority. These people are what evangelists often call "hot interests"— people whose hearts have already been prepared for the Adventist message. Others, like the poorer Thessalonians, may not be familiar with the Bible, yet when they're introduced to it, they find it fascinating because it speaks directly to their needs and concerns. You could say that God left footprints in the Thessalonian culture that the gospel would fill.* Before Paul arrived in the city, the Thessalonians

---

* Ellen G. White speaks about this in her book *The Desire of Ages* (Mountain View, Calif.: Pacific Press®, 1940), 31–38.

were prepared for the exact form and content of the gospel through the culture that had developed during the past two hundred years. Although the Thessalonians weren't acquainted with the Bible, the Cabirus cult prepared them to respond positively to Paul and his companions. However, it also incited the upper classes in the city to resist the gospel and to instigate riots.

There are also plenty of people like the Athenians whose hearts had to be opened through means other than the direct preaching of Scripture. Missionaries and evangelists who find themselves in such situations need to study the cultural environment, looking for points of contact between it and the gospel. Meeting people where they are usually means meeting them at some felt need. Everyone needs the gospel, but most people don't know that's what they're longing for. However, they do know they want a better marriage, a better job, a better way to handle money. They want healing for their ills; they want to learn how to raise responsible children; they want to feel they have value.

The Athenians felt that they needed answers to the great questions of life. The Thessalonian Jews longed for the coming of the Messiah. And the Thessalonian Greeks longed for deliverance from the oppression of Rome. Often, people become interested in the gospel when it's presented by Christians who have provided gracious, caring ministry at a point of felt need.

To the impatient evangelist, this kind of preparatory work may seem like a waste of time. "Spend your time on the people who are ready to make a decision for Christ," they often say. But everyone who is ready to make a decision has been through a process that has developed that readiness. Moving people along through that process is just as certainly authentic evangelism as altar calls and appeals for decisions are. When the needs people are most aware of are met, they're likely to discover the deeper needs they have, and it is then that they're most open to the gospel.

Throughout Scripture, God is pictured as meeting people where they were. Missionaries testify that God was present in the culture to which they were sent *before* they arrived there. When we meet people where they are, we are walking in the footsteps of God. Paul used this approach almost two thousand years ago, and we can use it too.

---

1. Ellen G. White, *Selected Messages,* vol. 1 (Washington, D.C.: Review and Herald®, 1958), 19–22; emphasis added.

2. White, *The Desire of Ages* (Mountain View, Calif.: Pacific Press®, 1940), 34.

3. Dio Chrysostom, *Discourses* 32.11, 12.

4. Robert Jewett, *The Thessalonian Correspondence: Pauline Rhetoric and Millenarian Piety* (Philadelphia: Fortress Press, 1986), 132.

CHAPTER 4

Greetings and Thanksgivings
(1 Thessalonians 1:1-10)

From this point on, I will begin each chapter of this book with my translation of the passage that will be the focus of that chapter. I've put the translations in verse format so as to expose, where possible, the structure of the Greek grammar and the relationships between the words. Where relevant, I have underlined the main sentence (subject and verb). I have also italicized the translation of participles that introduce major subordinate clauses or sentences. Because I have attempted to preserve the word order and language of the original, the English translation will occasionally be awkward. You will find it helpful to examine the translated passages carefully and to compare them with other translations before you read the comments that follow.

1 Thessalonians 1:1–5

1Paul, Silvanus and Timothy,
    to the church of the Thessalonians
        in God the Father and
        the Lord Jesus Christ,
  grace to you
    and peace.

²<u>We give thanks</u> to God all the time
 concerning all of you,
making mention of you in our prayers
 constantly
³*remembering* your
 work of faith and
 labor of love and
 patience of hope
  of our Lord Jesus Christ
 before our God and Father,
⁴*knowing,*
  brethren beloved by God,
 your election,
⁵because
 our gospel did not come to you
  in word only
 but also
  in power and
  in the Holy Spirit and
  in much certainty,
just as
 you know
  what we became among you
   for your sakes.

Paul, the primary author of the first letter to the Thessalonians (see 1 Thessalonians 2:18; 3:5; 5:27), opens the letter with greetings, as was the custom. If, as is commonly assumed, the Gospel of Matthew was written after the Thessalonian letters, the greeting at the opening of 1 Thessalonians contains the earliest written use of the word *church* in the New Testament. The church is made up of those who are "in God the Father and the Lord Jesus Christ." It is unclear whether the word *in* represents agency, meaning that God and Jesus created the church, or location, meaning that the church is wherever humans are in relation to God and Jesus.

After greeting the members of the church in Thessalonica, Paul tells them about his prayers on their behalf. In the Greek, verses 2–5 make up a single sentence, the main point of which is "we give thanks." The rest of the sentence describes how and why Paul and his companions are giving thanks. Prayer is never truly complete unless it is combined with thanksgiving. In verses 3–5, Paul introduces the whys of his thanksgiving with the words *remembering, knowing,* and *because.* Verses 6–10 elaborate further on what Paul says in verse 5.

Paul and his companions thank God that there is abundant evidence the Thessalonians are being faithful to God, specifically pointing to the church's faith, love, and hope. For Paul, this is not theoretical evidence; it is practical in the extreme. The evidence of faith is hard work. The evidence of love is labor and toil. The evidence of hope is a patient steadiness that puts up with current unattractive realities as the believers look to a bright future.

There is an interesting play on words in verse 5 that I couldn't translate into English. The Greek word translated as "come" in the first line is not the usual word for "come." In fact, the very same word is translated as "became" toward the end of the verse. This word contains the idea of a process or "becoming." The point is that Paul's gospel wasn't canned or static; it "became" something fresh in the context of Thessalonica. Because the gospel was shared there, both the preachers and those who listened were changed. In light of what Paul and his missionary companions suffered in Philippi, they had every reason to be fearful when they arrived in Thessalonica. Instead, they "became" confident, filled with the power of the Holy Spirit, and that power seeped over into the lives of the believers in Thessalonica as well.

1 Thessalonians 1:6–10

⁶And <u>you became imitators</u>

of us and
of the Lord;
having received the word
in spite of much affliction
with joy from the Holy Spirit,
[7]so much so that
<u>you have become</u> a model
to all who believe
in Macedonia
and Achaia,
[8]for
the word of the Lord has rung out
from you
not only in Macedonia and Achaia, but
in every place
your faith has gone out,
so much so that
we have no need
to talk about it,
[9]for
they themselves report
concerning you
what kind of access
we had with you,
and
how you turned
toward God
(and away from idols)
to serve the living and true God
[10]and
to await His Son
from heaven,
the One who arose

from the dead,
Jesus,
the One who rescues us
from the coming wrath.

In the Greek, verse 6 begins with the word *and,* making verses 2–10 a single compound sentence that gives the grounds for Paul's prayer of thanksgiving. Then, in verses 6–10, Paul is continuing to list the reasons why he is thankful to God for the Thessalonian believers. These reasons center on two realities about the Thessalonian church: first, it was imitating both Jesus and the apostles; and second, it had become a model for new believers everywhere.

In verse 5, the focus was on Paul and his companions, on the way God used them to bring the gospel to Thessalonica. In verse 6, the focus moves to the Thessalonians themselves. Paul continues to use the language of "becoming," using it now to talk about the spiritual development of the church. He is thankful that the Thessalonian believers have become imitators both of the apostles and of Jesus. Imitation is a major part of mentoring and discipleship.

Both the apostles and the Lord suffered unjustly, yet they experienced joy in the midst of suffering (1 Thessalonians 2:1, 2; Hebrews 12:1, 2). The fact that the Thessalonians were having the same experience was for Paul further evidence that they were growing spiritually. Before he had gotten news about them, he had been worried about their spiritual condition (1 Thessalonians 3:1–8). The report of their faithfulness drew from him the paean of praise and thanksgiving to God with which he began the letter.

The Thessalonians were not growing in faith merely for their own sakes, however; they were already taking leadership in the work of spreading the gospel throughout Greece and beyond (1 Thessalonians 1:7, 8). Remarkably, within a few months of their conversion, they had become leaders as well as disciples. (How likely is it that we would ordain as elders people who had been members of the church for only six months?) In an environment of persecution and suffering, God can spiritually grow people at a remarkable rate.

The Thessalonians shared the gospel in the context of the story of their own journey from idolatry to the worship of the true and living God (verses 9, 10). When Paul and his companions came to their city, the Thessalonians didn't let the hostility of their neighbors turn them away from the gospel; instead, they opened themselves to the apostles, the Holy Spirit, and the message they bore. The resultant changes in their lives were so exciting that, within six months, Paul could say that everyone had heard about it (verses 7, 8).

I'm going to address the two main elements of this chapter in more depth, but first I'll comment on another element. A major focus of both Thessalonian letters is the return of Christ (especially 1 Thessalonians 4:13–18; 5:1–11; 2 Thessalonians 1:5–10; 2:1–12), so, multiple minor references to the Second Coming are scattered throughout the two letters. The first of these references is in 1 Thessalonians 1:3. Paul often mentions the trio of faith, hope, and love, and when he does, he puts the attribute that's most important to the passage in last place. Thus, in 1 Corinthians 13:13, where Paul lists faith, hope, and love, he writes, "the greatest of these is love" (NIV). But in 1 Thessalonians 1:3—where he places the three in a different order: the "work of *faith* and labor of *love* and patience of *hope*"—the greatest of these is hope (emphasis added). Paul makes another reference to the Second Coming at the end of the chapter, speaking of Jesus as "the One who rescues us from the coming wrath" (verse 10). As the Thessalonian believers grew spiritually, they lived their lives in view of the Second Coming.

The connecting power of thankful prayer

One of the two most powerful themes in 1 Thessalonians 1 is that thankfulness expressed in prayer connects believers with each other. Thankfulness directs our attention away from ourselves to others. Paul didn't pray primarily for himself; rather, he prayed on behalf of others. His prayers were a form of what we sometimes call intercessory prayer.

At times, we're tempted to think of prayer as involving individuals and God. But 1 Thessalonians demonstrates that prayer can play an important role in drawing people together as a believing community. Intercessory prayer creates a triangle, connecting the person who prayed with God and with the community of faith, and as more and more members pray for each other, the church is bound ever more tightly in love and common concern.

How does this work?

For one thing, praying for others changes our attitude toward them. It's certainly difficult to sustain hard feelings toward someone we're praying for every day. When we seek God on behalf of those who dislike us, we receive a taste of His love for those who dislike Him. When we pray for someone to come to Christ and be forgiven, we become more aware that God has forgiven us. As we learn to pray for people who have hurt us, we experience God's forgiveness for the times we've hurt others. The kind of prayer that Paul was involved in as he prepared to write his first letter to the Thessalonians brings deep meaning and fulfillment to our lives. Let me share an example with you.

While I was traveling a few years ago, I decided to make a phone call to the pastor who had baptized me when I was twelve years old. As a child, I had always been in awe of him—he was such a man of God. While he was always earnest and serious, he exuded a quiet friendliness that attracted me to him. Now he was in his early eighties, retired, and living near the place where I was staying.

I placed the phone call, and, when he came on the line, I asked him what he was doing nowadays. I was totally unprepared for his answer.

"Nothing!" he said. "I do nothing! I *am* nothing. I'm like garbage! Every day I just sit around and do nothing, just waiting for tomorrow to come. Sometimes I go out into the garden for a half an hour or so, but otherwise I just sit and do nothing. I'm waiting for the Lord to take me home and give me rest."

I was stunned. I didn't know what to say. I sent up a quick prayer for guidance and then I got an idea. I asked him if he still prayed.

"Yes, of course," he said.

I asked him if he knew that intercessory prayer makes a difference.

"Yes, I suppose so," he said.

Then I asked him to pray for me and my ministry. I told him how much the prayers of others had helped my ministry. I told him that while the weakness of his body kept him from doing some things, he could still make a major difference. I told him that the administrators of the church were very busy people; they didn't have time to pray as much as they would like to. But he had time to pray. He could pray for the people who work at the General Conference—the Lord knows they can use all the help they can get! He could also pray for his conference president. I said perhaps God was keeping him alive because He needed him to pray for His cause in that area.

An amazing thing happened. As we talked about the possibilities, I detected a smile creeping into his voice. Then he became more and more excited, and his sense of hope began to grow stronger. He began to believe that the Lord was giving him time so that he could pray.

"When you become old, it's easy to feel as if your best days are behind you," I said. "But if God has kept you alive this long, maybe it's because your greatest days are still ahead of you! Maybe your conference has been dying for a lack of the prayers that only you can pray. Maybe you are the key to the work of God in this area!"

By the time that phone call was over, my former pastor wanted to continuing living. He was no longer waiting for the Lord to take him home; he now had a mission and a purpose. What a difference intercessory prayer can make!

We often skip over the first chapter of Thessalonians, thinking it contains mere formalities without a lot of content. We're eager to get to the "good stuff" in later chapters about the Second Coming and the events that lead up to it. But the opening chapter of 1 Thessalonians is as important as any other in terms of building up the church.

The path of spiritual development

My first senior pastorate was in a small-town church about a hundred miles northwest of New York City. The head deacon of the church was a man named Tom Kempton. He was a plumber by trade, but his hobby was working in a greenhouse he had built in his backyard. As the seasons came and went, he provided the appropriate plants for the church: Easter lilies for Easter, poinsettias for Christmas, brown and orange plants for Thanksgiving, and daffodils to celebrate the arrival of spring. The church was always beautifully decorated, and Tom let people take the plants home with them when the season ended.

Tom particularly delighted in Pamella—the lovely young woman who happened to be the pastor's wife. (Do you remember the story in chapter 1?) He often brought extra plants just for her. But Pamella had a hard time keeping plants alive back then, not having had much experience with them. We still laugh about the day when Tom came up to her with a twinkle in his eye and asked, "Do you need any more plants to kill?"

Today, much training and experience has turned Pamella into a plant doctor. She has planted more than forty species in our yard, and there are some forty or fifty plants inside the house as well, including orchids that are constantly blooming and a fifteen-foot-tall ficus tree, neither of which are easy to keep alive indoors. Obviously, Pamella knows a lot more about horticulture now. One of the painful lessons she learned in our first pastorate was that plants must grow and change or they will die. In chapter 3 of this book, I pointed out that Paul found that the gospel needed to be accommodated to the various cultures and contexts he encountered. Churches that are confronted by changing cultures have an opportunity to grow spiritually and theologically. Unfortunately, however, instead of taking advantage of that opportunity, many of them demand the end of all change. When they do that, they begin to die, whether or not their decline is noticeable at the time.

Paul measured the growth of the Thessalonian church on the basis of reports he received from Timothy. Are there contemporary ways to measure spiritual growth? People have produced a whole body of literature on the subject. The approach I've found the most helpful was recommended by Skip Bell of Andrews University. It's found in the book *The Critical Journey,* by Janet Hagberg and Robert Guelich.[1]

In what follows you will note significant differences from Hagberg. I've thought her system through and evaluated it by my personal experience, my experience as a mentor, and my study of the Bible and the Spirit of Prophecy, so what I offer here is both dependent on others and in some ways uniquely my own perspective. There are six stages in all, with some points of transition.

1. The acquaintance with God stage. I sometimes call this the romance stage. It is the time when the new believers are enjoying the spiritual "first love" experience—when they're feeling the great joy of walking with God. However, while the spiritual novices experience great joy, they don't yet know a lot about spiritual life, so they're vulnerable to superstition. The key at this stage is connecting the new believers with a community that can nurture and train them in a healthy way.

2. The learning or discipleship stage. At this stage, new believers explore, study, and learn how to fit into their new spiritual community. Finding the right mentor is crucial, as the new believers are eager to learn and can quite easily be led astray. People at this stage tend to have a great deal of confidence, feeling that they have found the truth, and they can become somewhat legalistic and inflexible.

3. The success stage. People who find a healthy mentor will grow, progressing from being disciples to being leaders. In this stage, believers help others learn what they have learned. Often, their leadership is praised and rewarded, and they feel confident and feel that they have arrived—that they've reached the pinnacle of what people expect from spiritual growth and leadership. If things ended right here, everyone would be happy. But that isn't what happens.

At some point in the third stage—usually when they're somewhere between the ages of thirty and fifty—most people of faith experience what I call the "dark night of the soul." This is a personal crisis in which past certainties become inadequate and they begin to question everything they've ever believed, and they find God to be silent or distant. This frightening experience needn't be destructive. The doubt these believers feel can lead to greater faith because it strips away the subtle selfishness that permeated them while they were in the success stage.

4. *The journey inward stage.* Some people back away from the dark night stage as if it wasn't from God, and some others blame their spiritual communities for all that seems to be going wrong. But those who accept this suffering as God's will for them will move into the fourth stage, the journey inward. Up to this point, believers have accepted the purpose of the church or their own ambitions as God's purposes for them, but the dark night drives them to understand and embrace what actually are God's unique purposes for their lives. Their faith moves from the head to the heart and becomes much more relational. The journey inward is like a second conversion.

5. *The journey outward stage.* At this stage, believers go back into the world and do the kinds of things they did in the success stage, but with different, more selfless motives. People will often change ministries at this stage and will become willing to take on smaller, humbler, and riskier tasks. They are now living to fulfill God's purposes rather than those of an institution, other people, or their own.

You would think that fellow church members would recognize and support those who are in this stage, whose spirituality is deepening. Surprisingly, though, the closer people come to God, the more out of touch they seem to be with those in the earlier stages. This often provokes a second dark night of the soul, which wrings more hidden selfishness out of their spirituality.

6. *The unconditional love stage.* Stage six followers of God are ruled by unconditional love. They have learned to see people through God's eyes and to love them the way God does. One would think people in this stage would be welcome in any religious institution, but they're not. Most people won't tolerate someone who loves their enemies, whether those enemies are abusers, people from different ethnic groups, annoying relatives, or church members with different points of view. So, unconditional love often proves disruptive to relationships.

By this time you probably wish I had stopped at stage three. We would love the ladder of faith to take us from triumph to triumph. But in this broken world, the closer we come to God, the stranger we become to other people—even when they are "in the faith." Paul experienced some of that estrangement in his relationship with fellow Jews in Thessalonica and with the church in Jerusalem (Acts 17:1–10; 21:17–36). That's what makes his letters so relevant to us today.

---

1. Janet Hagberg and Robert Guelich, *The Critical Journey: Stages in the Life of Faith,* 2nd ed. (Salem, Wis.: Sheffield Pub., 2005).

CHAPTER

The Example of the Apostles
(1 Thessalonians 2:1–12)

Two men trudged painfully down the dusty road. Ahead of them the sun was slowly moving toward the horizon. The Aegean breeze brought a small amount of relief at the end of a hot day.

Silas brushed a couple of flies away from his eyes. His ankles and wrists were sore, and his back was stinging where his tunic brushed against the wounds produced by the whipping he'd gotten in Philippi. Paul had also been beaten, and one of his eyes was black and his arms were bruised. It was time for them to reflect on what had happened to them.

"Why are we doing this?" Silas asked.

"Doing what?" Paul responded.

"Moving on to still *another* town, to preach the gospel again."

"I know what you mean. I sometimes wonder myself. But I just can't shake the conviction that everyone needs to know the Lord the way we know Him."

"Yeah, but why can't God send angels to do the job? I imagine no one would dare try to beat up an angel!"

Paul chuckled a bit at the thought, but stopped when the chuckling sent daggers of pain into his ribs.

"Paul, how do you *know* we're doing the right thing? I mean, I can put up with all kinds of pain and rejection when I know that I'm doing what God wants me to do. But what we're doing right now . . . I just don't know anymore."

Paul responded thoughtfully, "You're not the only one. I may seem to have it all figured out, but I have my moments too. I've found that my faith is strengthened when I review the prophecies of the Messiah and see how they come together in the life, death, and resurrection of Jesus. Nothing else and no one else but Jesus really fits those prophecies."

"You're totally right on that, Paul," Silas said. "I remember that when I first met Jesus in Jerusalem, I thought He was slightly crazy, like so many of the would-be preachers there. But as I listened to His words and then saw the events of that Passover weekend, the pieces started to fall together for me. This conviction came over me that what happened there was what Scripture was all about from day one! The Cross was God's greatest act of deliverance ever—greater than the Exodus, greater than the return from Babylon."

"That's right!" Paul said, excitement in his voice. "When you understand and receive Jesus, the Bible all fits together. It all makes sense."

Silas spoke up, taking the lead again. "I have to say though, Paul, that's only part of what keeps me going. When you commit yourself totally to gospel work, God steps in again and again, giving tokens of His approval. When we were in the stocks in that jail, I was feeling kind of down, just like now. I was wondering if we were ever going to see the light of day again. Then it hit me. *Sing!* It was almost as if God was commanding me. And when you joined in, our singing was the most beautiful sound I ever heard. It was as if the angels themselves were singing. Do you remember how the sound echoed around the jail cells?"

"How could I forget?"

"It was like a fire had been kindled inside of me," Silas said, "a joy I could never describe in mere words but I could express through singing. Even before the earthquake, I *knew* God was with us there, but after the earthquake—"

"Did you see the look on the jailer's face when he was running around, wondering where everyone went?" Paul said, interrupting. At that, both men burst out laughing—and then doubled over in pain. "It hurts, but I can't stop laughing!" Paul choked out.

When they had recovered, Silas spoke again, "Paul, how could I ever have doubted our mission? Feelings are such uncertain things; we're up one minute and down the next. I'm glad Scripture is solid even when I'm not."

Paul agreed. "Apostles are as human as anyone else," he said. "To stay on track, I need fresh assurance every day, every hour. I'm glad you brought it up, Silas; it helps when we share our struggles and our feelings. We can remind each other and encourage each other."

"Right!" Silas said.

"When you put it all together," Paul said, "it's perfectly clear that God is with us in this mission. This is where we're supposed to be and what we're supposed to be doing. I really couldn't live with myself if I didn't continue."

"Me either. What's Thessalonica like?"

"It's a free city under Roman rule. Maybe the people there will be more open than the Philippians were."

"Maybe. Well, it's on to Thessalonica then."

1 Thessalonians 2:1, 2

¹For <u>you yourselves know,</u> brothers,
    that our access with you
    was not empty,
²on the contrary
having suffered beforehand and
having been severely mistreated
    in Philippi,
    as you know,

<u>we began to be bold</u>
> through our God
> > to speak to you
> > > the gospel of God
> > > in the context of much inner struggle.

In 1 Thessalonians 2:1–12, we catch a glimpse of the inner life of Paul and his companions. Paul bares his soul for the benefit of the Thessalonians and, by extension, us. He challenges us to respond to our spiritual hopes, dreams, and motivations in ways that will please God and help others. In chapter 1, Paul told what others knew about the Thessalonians; here he tells what the Thessalonian believers themselves know.

The word translated as "access" picks up on the use of the same word in 1 Thessalonians 1:9. This word conveys the idea of welcome—the Thessalonians welcomed the apostles in spite of their injuries. Their minds and hearts were open to new truth. Perhaps sensing this, the apostles in turn became "bold" (1 Thessalonians 2:2). The word translated as "bold" corresponds to the word translated as "access"; they are like two sides of the same coin. The Thessalonians were open, and in return, the apostles felt free to speak. It was the ideal evangelistic situation. In chapter 3 of this book, we explored some of the historical reasons why the Thessalonians were so open to new ideas at this time.

1 Thessalonians 2:3–8

³For our appeal to you does not arise
> out of delusion or
> out of uncleanness or
> to deceive,
⁴on the contrary
> just as we have been tested (approved)
> > by God
> > to be entrusted

with the gospel,
just so do we speak,
not to please people
but God
who tests our hearts.
⁵For <u>we never came (became)</u> to you
with a word of flattery,
as you know,
nor with a motive of greed,
God is witness,
⁶nor seeking glory
from men
nor from you
nor from others,
⁷*being able* to "throw our weight around"
as apostles of Christ.
Instead <u>we became</u>
gentle in your midst
like a nursing mother
caring for her own children,
⁸thus
being kindly disposed toward you
<u>we thought</u> it well
to deliver to you
not only the gospel of God
but even our very souls
because you had become beloved
to us.

In this passage, Paul explains why he does what he does. What motivations drive someone to risk life and limb in order to share the gospel? It was widely known in the ancient world that money, sex, and power motivate much of human behavior. In the first century

A.D., many people took up preaching on the streets as an alternative to earning their living by performing hard labor. Others took to street preaching when they found that women were attracted to articulate men who were in the public eye. Still others reveled in the power over others that preaching great ideas gave them. But people who are motivated by money, sex, or power aren't motivated by the desire to please God. The two kinds of motivation are at odds with each other.

In the ancient world, orators knew that persuasive speech has three major components. People judged the power of an argument by the character of the speaker, the logic of the argument, and the quality of the appeal to the emotions or self-interest. In 1 Thessalonians 2:3–6, Paul focuses on the character of the apostles as a key element in their preaching. Paul's motivations were different than those of other preachers the Thessalonians may have known. If he had been motivated merely by money, sex, or power, the trouble he had experienced in Philippi would have made him quit.

In verse 3, Paul mentions three motivations people have for preaching. The first is best translated as "error," or "delusion"—an intellectual mistake. A preacher may be excited about an idea that is simply wrong. The second word is best translated as "uncleanness" or "impurity." The implication here is that some people preach because of the sexual opportunities that fame or notoriety brings. The third word is best translated as "deception" or "trickery." In this case, the speaker is aware that the ideas he presents are wrong, but he is consciously trying to mislead people in order to benefit himself.

Paul recognized that sinful human beings can't easily slough off the vices listed in verse 3. So, according to verse 4, he submitted himself to rigorous testing from God. That testing maintained his integrity and his intentions. Paul didn't want to distort the gospel by living a life that contradicted what he taught. He knew that God is the only Person worth pleasing and that God's approval was the source of his strength.

The Thessalonian letters make it clear that Paul modified his message to fit the audiences he addressed. While he was confident in God that he did so "for the sake of the gospel" (1 Corinthians 9:23, NIV), these changes left him open to the charge of pleasing people rather than God (verses 19–23). But meeting people where they are isn't necessarily wrong. Whether or not it's spiritually acceptable depends on one's motive. Paul met people where they were for the sake of the gospel, not for his own personal gain.

In 1 Thessalonians 2:5, 6, Paul lists three more temptations that preachers face. He denies using flattery, thus picking up again the theme of pleasing people. He also denies being motivated by covetousness— the desire for money and what it can buy. And he says that he wasn't motivated by the desire for praise from other people. As in verse 3, two statements about falsehood, in differing forms, sandwich one about lust—this time, lust for money. The bottom line of verses 3–6 is that Paul didn't exploit his audience for his own advantage, and his authenticity is safeguarded by his continual awareness that God sees him.

In verse 7, Paul asserts his right to the status of an apostle, which means he has authority over others and has the right to be paid. But the potential for misunderstanding (verses 3–6), combined with his great love for the Thessalonians (verse 8), caused him to take a different course with them. Paul declined that which was rightfully his to avoid putting a stumbling block in the path of his converts. This highlights an interesting feature of Paul's character and personality. While in his letters Paul could be demanding (e.g., see 2 Corinthians 10–13), in person, he seems to have been quite mild. He showed remarkable flexibility in his dealings with the Thessalonians, adjusting his approach to their needs and expectations. He used the gentleness of a nursing mother as an analogy for the way he treated them (1 Thessalonians 2:7).

1 Thessalonians 2:9–12

⁹For <u>you remember,</u> brothers,
    our labor and toil:

working night and day
    in order not to be a burden
      to any of you
<u>we preached</u> to you
    the gospel of God.
[10]<u>You are</u> witnesses and
<u>God is</u> also,
    how holy and
    righteous and
    blameless
<u>we became</u> among you who believe,
[11]just as <u>you know,</u>
    how <u>we dealt</u> with each of you
    like a father with his children,
      [12]*exhorting,*
      encouraging, and
      affirming you
        in order that you might walk worthy of God
        who calls you
          into His kingdom and
          glory.

In these verses Paul elaborates on the themes he has just introduced. Instead of accepting compensation for his gospel work, Paul labored every spare moment so as not to be a burden to his hearers. They are witnesses to both the blameless behavior of the missionary party and the parental concern they manifested toward the Thessalonians.

In this chapter's passage, 1 Thessalonians 2:1–12, Paul seems to enjoy expressing himself in threes. He did this twice in verses 3–6, describing the kinds of motivations he and the other apostles avoid. And verse 10 offers a trio of adjectives describing their behavior. It was "holy"; in other words, pleasing to God. It was "righteous"; they live in accord with human laws and social standards. And it was "blameless"; the apostles' actions were what both God and the Thessalonians would recognize as right and appropriate.

In verse 12, Paul uses another trio of Greek words to describe his ministry for the Thessalonians. He exhorts them—the Greek word has the basic meaning of "calling to one's side" and has connotations of *summons, appeal, request, encouragement,* and *consolation.* He encourages them—a Greek word that also has connotations of cheering up and comforting. And he affirms them—a translation of the Greek word for witness. To affirm someone is to offer testimony about the positive things he or she has done. This is the task of a father. Fathers appeal, summon, encourage, comfort, and affirm. For the most part, Paul doesn't mention the disciplinary side of the father's work. He does his disciplining in his letters; his personal touch was gentler. For Paul, to minister is to speak what you truly believe, to let God test your inner life and motivations, to always seek to please God, to be gentle and caring, and to allow positive emotional bonds to develop between yourself and the people to whom you are ministering. Paul does note a tension in ministry between being authentic and being all things to everyone. Authenticity may call us to speak plainly and forcefully, yet we must realize when people are not yet ready for that authentic message (John 16:12). Both authenticity and sensitivity are needed.

Steps to authenticity

How can we "get real" with God and with other people? In 1 Thessalonians 2, we catch a glimpse of Paul's rigorous "authenticity project." He laid himself bare before God's searching eye continually, lest having preached to others, he himself might become "disqualified for the prize" (1 Corinthians 9:27, NIV). What can we do to become more "real," more authentic, in our world today?

1. Spend time with the Word of God. The Bible aids our search for authenticity by affirming our value before God. As you read, mark the passages that tell how much God values us. Many of us have been raised in legalistic settings in which people affirm the gospel by what they say, but their lives deny its power. It is imperative that we saturate ourselves in the biblical texts that affirm the gospel until every legalistic doubt in our minds is driven away. Only when we know and understand the gospel will we have the courage to become self-aware.

The Bible's biographies—its stories about its major characters—offer further help as we search for self-awareness. Character after character is portrayed authentically; the people in the Bible are real people with significant flaws. In fact, many Bible heroes seem faultier than most of us are. Yet God used them in spite of their flaws. This characteristic of the Bible is powerfully described in one of the most remarkable passages in Ellen G. White's writings (see her *Testimonies for the Church,* 4:9–11.)[1] An honest reading of the Bible encourages authenticity and gives us the courage to confess our sins. That God could accept people such as Elijah, David, Peter, and Paul assures us that He can accept us too.

2. Practice authentic prayer. A crucial companion to authentic Bible study is authentic prayer—prayer that is directed toward God in full commitment. It is whole-hearted, whole-souled immersion in the prayer experience. Authentic prayer says, "I want the truth, no matter what the cost." When you tell God, "I want the truth, no matter what the cost," you will receive it, but you will also pay a price. Truth can cost you your family, your job, and your reputation. It can even cost you your life. Do you want to know the truth no matter what it may cost? If you do, God will reveal it to you.

But truth can be rather abstract. Learning the truth can mean gaining a correct understanding of all the beasts of Revelation or just the right sequence of steps people should take to come to God. Knowing doctrinal truth can be very satisfying, but it can also become a substitute for a more practical kind of truth. Knowing the truth about ourselves is very different from knowing abstract truth; it's seeing ourselves as other people see us, without the prejudices that normally skew our view of ourselves. Knowing ourselves this way calls for an even deeper level of authentic prayer. It means praying something like this: "Lord, I want the truth about myself no matter what the cost. Help me to see myself as other people see me." If you are willing to pay the cost, you can know the truth about yourself to the degree that you are ready for it (John 16:12).

3. Use some form of journaling. A close companion to authentic prayer is journaling. When I journal, God uses the writing process to draw up the depths of my being in ways that nothing else can. I can use journaling to pray, to record God's answers to prayer, and to take note of the various ways in which God has been at work in my life. In our search for authenticity, it is particularly helpful to invite God to probe whatever areas of our lives He wishes to examine and to expose us to it in what we write!* Many of the greatest Christians of all time, Ellen G. White among them, have practiced journaling as a tool of self-awareness.

4. Establish some system of accountability. The deepest level of the journey toward authenticity is accountability. Self-deception is rooted so deeply within each of us that it is intertwined even with our prayer lives and our Bible studies. Sometimes the only way that God can break through to us is through another human being. Ellen G. White noted this: "There are souls perplexed with doubt, burdened with infirmities, weak in faith, and unable to grasp the Unseen; but a friend whom they can see, coming to them in Christ's stead, can be a connecting link to fasten their trembling faith upon Christ."[2]

Accountability means allowing other people to help you keep watch over yourself. There are a number of ways that you can take advantage of this. One way is through a sharing group like Alcoholics Anonymous, where the only thing for which people are penalized is inauthenticity—hiding who they really are. Everyone is required

---

* For a detailed description of different types of journaling, see my book *Knowing God in the Real World: How to Have an Authentic Faith in a Faithless Society* (Nampa, Idaho: Pacific Press®, 2001).

to tell the truth about themselves and is accepted when they tell it. As you hear other people telling the truth about themselves, you recognize yourself in their confessions.

I have an even scarier suggestion for the brave few. Find a tough-minded friend who cares deeply about you—someone who would never want to see you hurt. Go to this friend and tell him or her, "If you knew that I wouldn't get mad at what you say and take it out on you later, what is there about me that you would tell me? What problems do you see in my relationship with God? How do I come across to other people?" The revelation that follows can be painful, but it is extremely helpful.

What if you don't have any close friends? What if you don't know anyone whom you would trust enough that you would be willing to tell the deepest anguish of your heart? Then find a good Christian counselor to help you. Counselors are trained to help people open up and discover the deeper truth about themselves. They are trained to be good listeners. Often they can detect when you are playing games of self-deception. While counseling can be helpful for everyone, it is particularly critical for those who have nowhere else to turn. Life is too short to waste in living inauthentically.

In 1 Thessalonians 2:1–12, we catch a glimpse of the inner life of the apostle, which is rare in the New Testament. It inspires a level of authenticity that we have rarely emphasized. It is one of the features of the Thessalonian letters that makes them uniquely valuable guides for the lives we live today.

---

1. Ellen G. White, *Testimonies for the Church* (Mountain View, Calif.: Pacific Press®, 1948), 4:9–11.

2. White, *The Desire of Ages*, 297.

Friends Forever
(1 Thessalonians 2:13-3:13)

Paul began his first letter to the Thessalonians with a prayer of thankfulness to God for the way these new converts had responded to the gospel (1 Thessalonians 1:1–10). He then reminded them of the two key motivations that energized his ministry: the desire to please God and the great bond of love that connected his heart with theirs (1 Thessalonians 2:1–12).

In the passage that this chapter focuses on (1 Thessalonians 2:13–3:13), Paul discusses the reasons he had to leave the city so suddenly and some of the events that occurred between then and the writing of his letter (see also Acts 17:1–18:11). A major theme of the whole section is friendship. The Thessalonians weren't just church members; they were also Paul's friends. A deep, emotional bond bound them together.

The depth of Paul's bond with the Thessalonians that we see in this passage is impressive. But their friendship is deeper than mere earthly friendships; it is a forever friendship that extends beyond the boundaries of time and this earth. Paul is looking forward to spending eternity with the Thessalonian believers (1 Thessalonians 2:19, 20; 3:13). We see throughout this letter that he had an intense concern regarding their beliefs and behavior. It was his hope for eternity that drove this concern.

Friends Forever (1 Thessalonians 2:13-3:13)

In chapter 2 of this book, we examined the seven stages of a relationship. Moving through these stages, especially the later, deeper stages, normally takes two people a considerable amount of time. Paul's relationship with the Thessalonians seems to have moved past the head and into the heart in less than three weeks. As we saw in the previous chapter, there is a depth of authenticity and openness in Paul's writing that is breathtaking when considered in light of how little time they were together. Paul was very open regarding his inner struggles, and he directly confronts the misunderstandings that may have arisen between him and them. Paul's relationship with the Thessalonians was not merely one he put on for the sake of evangelism. He intends to continue being close to his converts throughout eternity.

1 Thessalonians 2:13–16

[13]For this reason also
we give thanks to God constantly,
   because
       having received the Word of God
          which you heard from us
          which is from God
       you received it
          not as the word of men
       but
          as it truly is
          the Word of God,
             which is working
                in you who believe.
[14]For you, brothers, have become imitators
     of the churches of God
       which are in Judea
         in Christ Jesus,
 because
     you yourselves suffered the same things

from your own countrymen
just as
they did from the Jews,
15who *killed* the Lord Jesus and
the prophets and
drove us *out* (of Thessalonica) and
are not *pleasing* to God and
[are] hostile to all men,
16*hindering* us
to speak to the Gentiles
in order that they might be saved,
in order that they might fill up
the measure of their sins always.
The <u>wrath has come</u> upon them
to its completion.

At first glance, 1 Thessalonians 2:13–16 appears to be a digression from the topic. However, verse 13 ties this section with the preceding one (1 Thessalonians 2:1–12). It reminds readers of the Thessalonians' response to Paul's mission to them. First Thessalonians 2:14–16, then, sets the stage for what follows: a discussion of the reasons Paul had to leave Thessalonica so suddenly and all of the things that happened to him after he left.

Verse 13 states clearly that the words that Paul the apostle spoke to the Thessalonians were truly the Word of God to them. Thus, they experienced firsthand the developing canon of Scripture with which we are familiar. Paul preached to them from the Old Testament (Acts 17:2, 3), and Silas, a church leader from Jerusalem (Acts 15:22, 27), no doubt passed along oral recollections of what Jesus said and did when He was on earth. These oral recollections ultimately found their way into the written Gospels we have today.*

---

* Of course, Paul's words as passed along to us in his letters have also become a crucial part of the inspired Word of God that we treasure today.

Friends Forever (1 Thessalonians 2:13-3:13)

In 1 Thessalonians 2:14–16, Paul was letting the Thessalonians know that they were not the only ones who were suffering persecution from their neighbors. Christians in Judea had been suffering in the same way ever since the church came into existence. The vehemence of Paul's language with regard to the Jews in these verses has troubled many recently, particularly in light of the Holocaust that took place in the middle of the twentieth century. What Paul wrote is more understandable when we realize that his target was the Judean authorities who killed Jesus, persecuted the earliest Christians, and then followed Paul around, obstructing his preaching of the gospel wherever they could, including in Thessalonica (Acts 17:5). Paul the apostle was human; he had feelings and frustrations like the rest of us.

We must also remember the larger context of this statement. Paul lived in a world in which the followers of Jesus were a persecuted minority. The Jewish leadership, which should have been an ally of the Christians, instead often sided with the oppressive majority in order to gain political advantage over this subgroup that was growing among them. In today's world, the situation is often reversed. Particularly in Europe during the past century, Jews suffered greatly at the hands of supposedly Christian governments. The universalization of Paul's words during the Holocaust was very un-Christlike and very damaging. Words and ideas change in meaning over time. Simply repeating Paul's words without qualification can have consequences Paul never intended. Prejudice against whole classes of people is not appropriate for those who live at the foot of the cross. As Paul himself notes twice, we should think of others as souls "for whom Christ died" (Romans 14:15, NKJV; 1 Corinthians 8:11, NKJV).

Reading this passage in light of the larger picture of Paul's attitude toward the Jews also helps us to understand it better. Paul wasn't attacking all Jews everywhere and all the time. After all, he himself was a Jew. We need to counterbalance what we read in

1 Thessalonians 2 with what we find in Romans 11. There Paul pours out his heart in love for his people. As long as there are Jews like Paul who follow Jesus as their Messiah, we can know that God has not rejected His people, the Israel of the Old Testament (Romans 11:1, 2). God was still using them—His grace had moved Him to choose a remnant of Jews to join Paul in the practice and proclamation of the gospel (verse 5).

Though most of the Jews of Paul's day rejected the gospel, Paul regarded that to be a strategic move through which God made room in the church for Gentiles (verse 11). Comparing the church to a tree, Paul pointed out that even if the vast majority of the branches of that tree were Gentiles, the roots and trunk of the tree were still Jewish (verses 17–24). Though Paul was committed to the Christian church, he didn't reject his own Judaism. Rather, he embraced it and expanded its reach. He had a magnificent vision of the "full inclusion" of the Jews at the very end of time (verses 12, 25–27). Romans 11 is a powerful testimony that God has not given up on His Jewish people. Paul didn't either (verses 1, 2, 29), and neither should we. Ellen G. White wrote,

> In the closing proclamation of the gospel, when special work is to be done for classes of people hitherto neglected, God expects His messengers to take particular interest in the Jewish people whom they find in all parts of the earth. As the Old Testament Scriptures are blended with the New in an explanation of Jehovah's eternal purpose, this will be to many of the Jews as the dawn of a new creation, the resurrection of the soul. As they see the Christ of the gospel dispensation portrayed in the pages of the Old Testament Scriptures, and perceive how clearly the New Testament explains the Old, their slumbering faculties will be aroused, and they will recognize Christ as the Saviour of the world. Many will by faith receive Christ as their Redeemer. . . .

Friends Forever (1 Thessalonians 2:13-3:13)

Among the Jews are some who, like Saul of Tarsus, are mighty in the Scriptures, and these will proclaim with wonderful power the immutability of the law of God.[1]

Notice that in verse 15, my translation reads "drove us out" instead of the King James Version's "persecuted." I translated it that way because Paul didn't use the Greek word usually translated as "persecute" (*diōkō*). Instead, he used a word that adds the prefix *ek*, "out"—*ekdiōkō*. This, then, isn't a reference to the persecution of Christians in Jerusalem, but to Paul's own experience of being "kicked out" of Thessalonica a few months before. The hostility of some Jews, exercised first in the crucifixion of Jesus and then in the persecution of the early church, had now also moved them to hinder the preaching of the gospel in Thessalonica.

1 Thessalonians 2:17–20

[17]But <u>we,</u> brothers,
    having been orphaned away from you
        for a short time,
        (in face, not in heart),
<u>made</u> every <u>effort</u>
    with great longing
    to see you face to face.
[18]Wherefore,
<u>we wished to come</u> to you,
    I Paul again and again,
but
<u>Satan thwarted</u> us.
[19]For <u>what is</u> our hope
    or joy
    or crown of boasting?
<u>Is it</u> not even you
    in the presence of our Lord Jesus

at His coming?
[20]For <u>you are</u> our glory
and our joy!

In the fourteen verses that run from 1 Thessalonians 2:17 through 3:10, Paul offers a chronological account of his separation from the Thessalonian believers. The theme of friendship runs throughout the passage. Paul wants the criticisms of the church and the advice he will give later (in chapters 4 and 5) to be read in the light of his deep love and concern for them. Advice is best received when it is grounded in a relationship.

Paul's absence from the Thessalonians is painful. It makes him feel like an orphan, and, as a result, he has made repeated efforts to get back to them. However, Satan has thwarted those efforts (1 Thessalonians 2:17, 18). In historical terms, the best explanation for how Satan blocked Paul's attempts to return involves the "bail money" the Thessalonian officials took from Jason and the believers (Acts 17:9). Had Paul returned at the wrong time, the new believers would probably have had to forfeit that money, which could well have impoverished them. Paul would have returned earlier if doing so would have threatened only his own well-being, but he saw no reason to endanger the young church just so he could satisfy his longing to be with them.

Paul seems to say quite clearly that it was Satan, not God, who prevented him from returning to Thessalonica. When the closing of a door has resulted in dire consequences, we can be quite sure that Satan was at work. And conversely, if the door being closed has resulted in blessings, we can recognize that God was behind it all. However, we must remember that in this life, we seldom see the whole picture. Eventually, life experience, a commitment to follow God's will for us, and an awareness of and a growing sensitivity to the voice of the Spirit may enable us to "read" the origins of the obstacles we come upon. But even when that's not the case, we can rest in the assurance that if we've put ourselves into God's hands, He'll make everything we face in life work together for good (see Romans 8:28).

Why does Paul have such a strong longing to see the Thessalonians? It's because he regards them as a validation of his ministry. When Jesus returns, the Thessalonians will be Paul's joy and his boast. He will be proud to show them off to Jesus. Paul wasn't content merely to be saved, he wanted evidence that he had been the means of blessing other people. Something about the Thessalonians assured him that they would stand firm until the end; they would be there for him when Jesus comes. While the church needed Paul, he also needed them!

1 Thessalonians 3:1–5

¹For this reason
　　being no longer *able to endure* it
we thought it well
　　to be left in Athens alone.
²So we sent Timothy,
　　our brother and
　　God's fellow worker
　　　　in the gospel of Christ,
　　in order to strengthen and
　　encourage you
　　　　with regard to your faith,
³so that no one might be shaken
　　by these afflictions.
For you yourselves know
　　that we are destined for this.
⁴For when we were with you,
　　we kept telling you
　　　　that we are about to be afflicted,
　　just as it happened and

71

just as you know.
⁵For this reason
    being no longer *able to endure*
  <u>I sent</u> in order to know your faith,
    lest in some way
      the tempter had tempted you and
      our work might have been in vain.

In 1 Thessalonians 3:2–4, Paul gives a number of reasons why he sent Timothy back to Thessalonica. The primary reason he gives in these verses is his desire to help them avoid being "shaken" by the suffering they were experiencing. He felt that Timothy's encouragement would see them through.

The word *shaken* in verse 3 is a translation of a Greek word used, for instance, of a dog "wagging" its tail. Afflictions can cause people to "shake"—in other words, to waver back and forth between commitment to God and spiritual uncertainty. Paul reminds the Thessalonians that their having to suffer affliction shouldn't surprise them. Matthew 24 tells us that Jesus had prophesied that His disciples would face affliction. We can handle suffering better when we see it as a fulfillment of Jesus' prophecy. In that case, it confirms the truth of what we have believed.

God hasn't given us prophecy just to satisfy our curiosity about the future. Rather, He means it to encourage us to stand firm. Prophecy helps us to endure by preparing us for afflictions before they come. If Paul couldn't go to Thessalonica to remind the new believers of these things, Timothy was certainly a good second choice.

1 Thessalonians 3:6–10

⁶But now Timothy,
    having come to us from you, and
    having reported to us
      your faith and love and

that you have a good memory
> of us
> > at all times
> > *desiring* to see us
> > > just as we also desire to see you,
>
⁷for this reason,
> brothers,
we have been comforted
> by you
> in all our distress and
> > difficult circumstances
> by means of your faith,
⁸because now we just might continue living,
> if you are standing fast
> > in the Lord.
⁹For what thanks could we give
> > to God
> > for you
> because of all our joy and rejoicing
> > in the presence of God
> > on account of you?
¹⁰Night and day we pray,
> as earnestly as possible,
in order that
> we might see each of your faces, and
> complete what is lacking
> > in your faith.

When Timothy returned, he reported the condition of the Thessalonian believers to Paul and told him that they had good memories of him and longed to see him. For whatever reason, Paul had refrained from corresponding with them up to this point, but now that he's heard Timothy's report, he decides to write. This passage comes closest to explaining why he had waited to write.

People tend to build a sense of self-worth on the basis of three things: possessions (the things they have), performance (how well they do things), and people (what others think of them). The gospel (what Jesus thinks of us) is the best foundation on which to build a stable sense of self-worth, but our fragile humanity craves these earthly tokens of success and the sense that others think highly of us.

The apostle Paul seems to have been no exception to this desire. In this passage, he reveals his hunger for the approval of the Thessalonians. To some degree, his sense of self-worth as a person was tied to the success of his mission endeavors. He rejoices not only in the news that they are standing fast in the Lord, which validates the success of his ministry, but also that they think well of him and long to see him as much as he longs to see them. It seems that Paul held off writing until he knew that his letter would be welcome! I can relate to that. In fact, I find it encouraging that even apostles can be concerned about what others think of them.

In 1 Thessalonians 3:7, Paul again picks up the language of the end-time Tribulation. The two words behind the phrase "distress and difficult circumstances" denote the sufferings of the end time (see also 1 Corinthians 7:26, 28). As I mentioned earlier, when people see the suffering they're experiencing in the light of prophecy and the end of time, it provides meaning and purpose—if not during the suffering, certainly afterward.

In 1 Thessalonians 3:9, 10, we gain further insight into Paul's prayer life. His prayers were filled with thanksgiving and rejoicing. Here, he also asks to see the Thessalonians and complete what is lacking in their faith. Through prayer, Paul brought the inner details of his life before the throne of God. It was through prayer that he processed his worries and his fears, his hopes and his joys. He could walk tall in the midst of affliction because he knew God as a Friend.

Thankfulness and joy are related. Thankfulness takes our minds off of ourselves and directs our thoughts toward God and others. A spirit of thankfulness brings a great deal of joy. Glenn Coon, one of my all-time favorite preachers, used to emphasize Nehemiah 8:10: "The joy of the LORD is your strength" (NKJV). He believed the secret of spiritual power is the joy that comes from a spirit of thankfulness and praise. We cannot stay sad for long when we are continually reciting the ways in which God has blessed and enriched our lives.

Coon suggested that we spend a little time each morning writing down ten things for which we are thankful. He said that then, during the course of the day, we should make each of these blessings the focal point of a brief prayer: "Thank You, Lord, for the air." "Thank You, Lord, for the cat [or the dog]." "Thank You, Lord, for the red roses." This kind of prayer gets into the very basics of life. It's very down-to-earth, practical stuff.

While Coon's strategy sounds simplistic and corny, I've found that it really works. It brings a sense of God's concern for every detail of life. Nothing can brighten our lives like having a spirit of thankfulness and praise. Paul seems to have made this a lifelong habit. No wonder he was able to endure so much suffering and still stay true to his mission!

1 Thessalonians 3:11–13

[11]Now may our <u>God and Father</u> Himself,
    and our Lord <u>Jesus,</u>
      <u>direct</u> our way to you;
[12]<u>may</u> the Lord <u>make</u> you <u>increase</u> and <u>abound</u>
    in love toward one another
    and toward everyone
just as
    ours does toward you,
      [13]in order to establish your hearts
        blameless in holiness,
          before our God and Father,

at the coming of our Lord Jesus Christ
with all His holy ones.

The Greek verbs in this passage are *optatives,* an unusual grammatical mood. In the New Testament, verbs in this form are used most frequently in "wish prayers," such as the one in the three verses above.

This prayer of Paul sounds a bit like the benediction at the end of a worship service. Paul was praying that the Thessalonians would increase in love both toward other members of the church and toward the wider society around the church. He wants the believers to love others just as the apostles have showered God's love upon them. The ultimate goal is that in the final judgment God will account the believers as blameless.

The second coming of Jesus is a powerful incentive to grow spiritually. At His coming, every act of abuse and oppression will be brought to justice, and every act of love and kindness will be recognized and rewarded (e.g., see Matthew 10:42). That means that every act in this life, no matter how small, has meaning in the ultimate scheme of things.

But Paul considered it equally important that the Second Coming will bring a glorious reunion of family and friends, whose relationships will last forever because of what Jesus has done. Christian relationships don't have an expiration date. They are designed to be eternal.

---

1. Ellen G. White, *The Acts of the Apostles* (Mountain View, Calif.: Pacific Press®, 1911), 381.

Practical Advice for Urban Christians
(1 Thessalonians 4:1-12)

The first three chapters of 1 Thessalonians are focused primarily on the past. Paul wrote about what happened during and after his first visit. In chapters 4 and 5, however, Paul turns from the past to the future. The faith of the Thessalonian believers was deficient in some ways (1 Thessalonians 3:10), and Paul wants to help them remedy these deficiencies. The letter would begin the process, but the project wouldn't be complete until Paul saw the Thessalonians in person again.

Paul's prayer in 1 Thessalonians 3:11–13 sums up the first three chapters of the letter, but it also anticipates the themes of chapters 4 and 5: "increase," "sanctification" (holiness), the Second Coming, and mutual love. The prayer is like a bridge that brings the Thessalonians, and later readers, to the points Paul now wants to make.

1 Thessalonians 4:1, 2
¹Finally therefore, brothers,
we ask you and
encourage you
in the Lord Jesus,
that as you have received

> from us
>> how it is necessary for you
>>> to walk and
>>> to please God,
>>>> as you are continually walking,
>> that you excel in this more and more.
> ²For <u>you know</u>
>> what sort of instructions
>>> we gave you
>>>> through the Lord Jesus.

With "finally therefore," Paul moves from the appetizer to the meat of practical Christianity. In a sense, the first two verses of chapter 4 are an introductory summary of the whole of chapters 4 and 5. Basically, Paul is encouraging the Thessalonians to continue—and increase—what they're already doing.

The word *walk* in verse 1 is translated from a Greek word, *peripateō,* that basically means "walking around." We get the English word *peripatetic* from this root. A person who is peripatetic spends a lot of time walking around. I may be one of those people—I can't stand being cooped up in an office all day. When I have a one-on-one appointment with someone, I often ask if they would mind taking a walk around the neighborhood while we talk. I find our minds work better and we accomplish more when we're walking than we would just sitting in the office.

But there's something extra in Paul's use of the term. In the ancient Hebrew language and culture, "walking around" was a metaphor for daily life. In verse 1, Paul connects walking with pleasing God. As the title of this chapter states, Paul gives lots of practical advice on how urban Christians should live. That advice is still valid today. In other words, this passage provides a window into the kind of practical training Paul gave to those who became Christians through his efforts. Our heavenly Father is pleased when our characters and behaviors resemble His character and behavior. When we are kind and gracious, we mirror the kind and gracious character of God. When we abstain from sexual immorality, we show respect for the value that God sees in other people, and He is pleased when we choose to value what He values.

The Thessalonians are already pleasing God by their behavior and character. In verse 1, Paul encourages them to do what they are already doing "more and more." The Christian life is to be an ever-growing relationship with God. This is realistic and practical. Paul knows that new believers cannot attain the heights of *sanctification*— a word he uses several times in this passage—overnight. It is truly "a battle and a march" that lasts a lifetime. Even seasoned believers are daily disappointed with some aspect or another of their behavior. So instead of telling us to focus on the occasional good deed or misdeed, Paul encourages us to pay attention to the trend of our lives, and to do this in the full assurance that God loves us like a mother loves her newborn child.

Good parents don't punish three-month-old children for not knowing how to walk. They encourage them to do what they can and to do it more and more. Over time, the children will learn to crawl and then to walk and then to run, and great is the rejoicing when this happens! "More and more" is the word!

Verse 2 is much easier to translate than is verse 1, but verse 2 contains one point of uncertainty: the question of what Paul meant when he wrote "through the Lord Jesus." What was his perception of the connection between his behavioral advice and Jesus? The Greek version of 1 Thessalonians reveals that Paul used multiple expressions that remind the knowledgeable reader of the sayings of Jesus in the four Gospels. Since it is likely that none of those Gospels had been written when Paul wrote to the Thessalonians, it seems probable that he learned what Jesus said from the disciples and other followers of Jesus. He would have used Jerusalem stalwarts such as Barnabas and Silas like reference books. While Paul may not have met Jesus in person during Jesus' earthly ministry (1 Corinthians 15:3–8), he was very attentive to the oral tradition that others had received and that would later be recorded in the four Gospels.

So, in chapters 4 and 5 of 1 Thessalonians, Paul was offering more than his own good advice. He was not only sharing his own theology with the Thessalonians, he was also passing along the tradition of Jesus' own words. Jesus Himself had called for the behaviors that Paul was encouraging. Thus, the teachings in our passage are given on the highest possible authority—the authority of the God who was made flesh.

1 Thessalonians 4:3–8

³For this is the will of God,
   your sanctification (holiness),
   to keep away
      from sexual immorality.
⁴To know (each of you)
      how to acquire his own vessel
         in holiness and honor,
      ⁵not in passion of lust
         like the Gentiles
            who don't know God:
⁶in order that no one
   transgress and
   defraud his brother
      in this matter
because <u>the Lord is</u> an avenger
   with regard to all these things,
   just as <u>we told</u> you and
      <u>warned</u> you ahead of time.
⁷For <u>God did</u> not <u>call</u> us to uncleanness
   but in holiness.
⁸Consequently, whoever rejects (this instruction)

does not reject man
but God
who gives His Holy Spirit to us.

The key word is this passage (verses 3–8) is "holiness," or "sanctification." This is God's will for us. Something becomes holy when it is dedicated, set apart, and consecrated for special use. The form of the word *holiness* that Paul uses is that of an action noun. Paul emphasizes the *process* of becoming holy rather than the result. What he means by sanctification in this context is explained by the clause that follows: to keep away from sexual immorality. Those who believe that Paul endorsed a law-free gospel will find 1 Thessalonians 4:3–8 to be a challenging text. Paul lays out some very strict behavioral requirements for those who are in Christ.

Verse 4 has long been a puzzle to students of the Bible. The phrase "acquire his own vessel" can mean at least two different things, so let's dig deep. The word translated as "acquire" is a verb that can focus either on the beginning of an action (acquire something you did not have before) or on a later stage of that action (maintain or control something you already have). The word translated as "vessel" can mean a body or person in general (see Acts 9:15, NKJV; Romans 9:21, NKJV; 2 Timothy 2:21, NKJV) or a woman in particular (the "weaker vessel," 1 Peter 3:7, NKJV). Thus, the two best translations are "acquire a woman [wife] for yourself" or "control your own body and/or your own sexual organs." Is his counsel very specific—that a man satisfy his sexual desire by acquiring a wife (see also 1 Corinthians 7:36–38)? Or is he just making the more general statement that we should control our sexual urges? The phrase could be read either way—and either way, the point is that Christians are not to relate to lustful passions the way most Gentiles did back then.

In verse 6, Paul introduces an idea that is unique within Scripture. He says that sexual immorality "defrauds" one's "brother." To defraud means to take advantage of or cheat someone; to take something that is not rightfully ours. The word is related to covetousness—wanting something that doesn't belong to us. For Paul, the best definition of "brother" is someone for whom Christ died (Romans 14:15; 1 Corinthians 8:11). "Brother" here would include anyone—male or female—who is affected by our sexual actions.

In this passage Paul is telling us something that the movie industry rarely does. He's saying that the very idea of "casual sex" is a fantasy. Promiscuous sex damages both parties deeply. We now know that the casual touching of someone's private parts in childhood can affect everything that person thinks and does throughout life. How much more, then, does the deep invasion of overt sexuality affect the very core of a person's being. A bonding between two people is implied that can never be merely casual. From that day forward, feelings are confused, and when they are suppressed, as they often are, they go on to do internal damage whether or not one is aware of it.

But more than this, promiscuous sex also defrauds the future spouse. He or she gets a partner who cannot bond fully because parts of that person's heart have been given away to others already. Marital bonding will be frustrated because one spouse's ability to love has been split off, causing relational confusion. Furthermore, although a spouse may forgive the other spouse's past, he or she will have a hard time fully trusting the partner. What has happened once can happen again. Thus, uncertainty and confusion are introduced into a relationship that should be unfettered by memories of indiscretions. The word Paul chose to use here, "defraud," is right on the mark of what we know about sexuality today.

But there is even more. In Matthew 25:40, the "brother" is also the "brother" of Christ. So the question of sex is not only about how we treat other human beings, but how we treat Christ in the person of that "brother." Sex is ultimately about one's relationship with God. The Gentiles, who do not know God, live lives of passionate lust (1 Thessalonians 4:5). It is ignorance of God that produces immoral behavior. Those who ignore the Bible's teachings on this subject reject not only those teachings, but also God Himself (verse 8; see also 1 Corinthians 6:19, 20). So, casual sex is not an option for Christians. On the other hand, however, when two people engage in sex according to God's design, it becomes a beautiful illustration of the self-sacrificing love that God poured out upon us in Christ (see John 13:34, 35). So, the question of how we relate to sex becomes the question of what we do with Christ in the person of the "brother."

While the saints should not be sexless, neither should sex be "saintless"! Sex is holy, set apart for marriage. The greatest joy known to human beings is found in the intimate freedom of sexuality enjoyed according to God's design.

The temptation of attraction

Why would any believer want to defraud another? Why would any committed spouse turn away from the object of his or her affection to seek the affection of another? (Readers who wish to avoid the rather frank portrayal of sexual temptation that follows may want to skip down to page 87 and begin reading again with my translation of the next section of Paul's letter, 1 Thessalonians 4:9–12.) I think the seriousness of what Paul wrote in verses 3–8 calls us to examine carefully what happens when Christians behave promiscuously.

Human sexuality is part of God's design. According to Genesis, God created men and women to be attracted to each other. To feel an attraction to a member of the opposite sex isn't a sin; it is a gift from God. Most people, if not all, are born with the capacity for some degree of attraction to members of the opposite sex. Experiences in life can either heighten or dampen this sense of attraction, but, to some degree, it is natural and inborn.

God designed sexuality for our benefit, but His enemy seeks to destroy that design, and the weapon he uses is called temptation. Every so often when you meet someone else, you feel a heightened sense of attraction. It doesn't matter that you are married before

God, the chemicals go to work, and you feel what people call "love at first sight." Being around this person to whom you are strongly attracted is not what the Bible calls sin, but how you handle the situation is critical. You've definitely come to a fork in the road. The wisdom of the world says, "Go for it." The Word of God counsels otherwise.

What would Paul tell you to do in such a situation? I don't think he would want you to deny the attraction and act as if it weren't there. It is safer to acknowledge what is happening and confront it by bringing it into your consciousness. Ask yourself why you are so attracted to this person. Do you have unmet needs? Are there issues you need to discuss with your spouse? Having previously given in to sexual temptation heightens one's sexual focus. Is that a factor here? As best as you can, use your reason to control your feelings. Finding someone—a fellow believer whom you trust—to be a partner who will hold you accountable can enhance the power of reason. Telling this person what you're feeling often takes a lot of the "adventure" out of the situation. Knowing that a friend is watching you can also make you feel foolish about the whole thing, which is closer to reality than the temptation is.

The most helpful action you can take is to count the cost carefully before you yield to such a temptation. Recognize that committing sexual sin displeases God (1 Thessalonians 4:1). It also betrays people whom you love (Genesis 39:8, 9; 1 Thessalonians 4:6), and it defrauds the person to whom you are attracted (1 Thessalonians 4:6). In addition, down the road it will bring major consequences to you as well (verse 6). A wise pastor wrote the following "note to self."

If I go farther down this road [of sexual temptation], I will probably grieve the One who redeemed me. I will probably drag His sacred name into the mud. . . . One day I will have to look Jesus, the righteous Saviour, in the face and give an account of my actions. If I go farther I will probably inflict untold hurt on my wife, who is my best friend and who has been faithful to me. I will lose my wife's respect and trust; I will hurt my beloved daughters. I will destroy my example and credibility with my children. I might lose my wife and my children forever. I could cause shame to my family. I could lose self-respect. I could create a form of guilt awfully hard to shake. Even though God would forgive me, would I ever be able to forgive myself? I could form memories and flashbacks that could plague future intimacy with my spouse. I could heap judgment and endless difficulty on the person with whom I committed adultery. I could possibly reap the consequences of diseases like gonorrhea, syphilis, herpes, or AIDS. Maybe I could cause a pregnancy, and that would be a lifelong reminder of my sin. Maybe I would invoke shame and lifelong embarrassment on myself.[1]

The two options look a little different from that perspective, don't they? But some Christians are ready to take risks for a little "fun."

What happens if you don't turn away from the sexual attraction? You begin to fantasize about that person, imagining what life would be like with her. You wonder if he feels as attracted to you as you are to him. You deliberately alter your route at the office to walk by her door so you can see her—see how she looks today. You learn his schedule and "just happen" to be around when he shows up.

You may think the world of fantasy is safe because no one knows you're living there (although, of course, God does). But even at the stage of fantasy, damage is being done. You are wasting time that would be better spent with your spouse or on your relationship with God. In addition, the more time you spend in fantasyland, the harder it is to enter into legitimate relationships. And since reality can never live up to fantasy, you are training yourself to fail in the relationships that matter the most. At this point you can still turn around, but many people move on to the next step.

That next step is flirtation. You say something to her that has a double meaning just to see how she will respond. You share confidences with him that you have no business sharing with an acquaintance. You allow your fingers to brush hers as you exchange a paper or object, hoping for a response that indicates she is as interested in you as you are in her. Sensing another person's attraction to you produces a thrill that calls for further contact.

Unless matters are arrested at this point, things can only move downhill from here. If you're a Christian, you'll probably have a hard time believing you could cross the line with someone other than your spouse, so at first you find legitimate excuses for being together, such as working on some project together or studying the Bible together. But deep down inside, it's the attraction that is the true motive for developing the relationship. Then fantasy starts to become reality, and you make a conscious decision to spend time with that person outside of the boundaries of God's design.

Sexual sin doesn't begin with fornication or adultery; that's where it ultimately takes a person. And when fantasy becomes a reality, it always has a bitter aftertaste. Movies and TV shows rarely show that. People who commit a sexual sin are deeply wounded by the experience, even when they deny it to others and to themselves. Take a tip from Paul; if you are playing with sexual temptation right now, stop, take a cold shower, memorize 1 Thessalonians 4:1–8, seek out a trusted friend, think through the consequences, and do whatever it takes to get out of that situation. If your fantasy has already become a reality, you have a long, hard road ahead of you; but you can break the relationship off, do what you can to make restitution to all individuals concerned (including doing your best for the baby, if it has gone that far), ask forgiveness of all who have been hurt by your actions, and throw yourself on the abundant mercy of God. Your life may never be the same, but you can do a lot to limit the damage.

1 Thessalonians 4:9–12

[9]Now concerning brotherly love
you have no need (for us) to write to you,
for you yourselves are taught
by God
to love one another,
[10]for that is indeed how you are behaving
toward all the brothers
throughout Macedonia.
But we urge you, brothers,
to do so more and more, and
[11]to aspire to live quietly, and
to mind your own business, and
to work with your own hands,
just as we instructed you,
[12]in order that you might walk properly
in relation to those who are outside, and
that no one might be in need.

The Greeks had a number of words for love, three of which are found in the New Testament. *Eros* is the Greek word from which we get the English word *erotic*. *Eros* refers to the sexual side of love. *Agapē* is the Greek word for love used most often in the New Testament. It refers to self-sacrificing love and is the word used of Christ's love for us as manifested at the Cross.

The third Greek word for love used in the New Testament is *phileō*. It's the word translated as "brotherly love" in the passage above. In the Gentile world, this word referred to people's love for their blood relations, but the church extended this meaning to love for fellow believers—the Christian family of choice. God calls for this kind of familial love, and whenever it happens, it's a miracle of His grace.

The opening phrase of the verse, "now concerning," suggests that

Paul wrote verses 9–12 in answer to questions the church raised with Timothy. They understood the principle of brotherly love but didn't know how to use that principle in real life. Paul gets specific in verses 10–12, telling the Thessalonians that they were to express brotherly love in three ways: they were to aspire to live a quiet life, they were to mind their own business, and they were to work with their hands. These three are all related. In the ancient world, manual labor was the primary means of self-support. The root of loving our "brothers" is to take care of ourselves first—carrying our own weight, making sure we aren't dependent on others. Enthusiasm for the second coming of Jesus may have led some of the Thessalonian believers to quit their jobs and become dependent on their Gentile neighbors. This would cause the Gentiles to consider them to be lazy and disruptive, expecting others to take care of them, and this perception would have brought the fledgling church into disrepute.

In today's world, Paul might advise, "Support yourself and your family, and save a little extra to help those in legitimate need." He also would probably say that being ready to witness at all times doesn't mean being disruptive, nosy, or lazy on the job. The only view of the church some outsiders will ever have is the impression they get from the behavior of the Christians they know in their everyday lives.

How do you live a quiet life in the midst of a city today? In 2006, I returned to New York City to attend a class. Having grown up there, I looked forward to the three-week-long intensive class, which was to be taught in a room within a block or two of Times Square, at the very heart of Manhattan. We estimated that about twenty thousand people an hour walked by on the sidewalk outside the classroom. What struck me most about the people hurrying by on their way to somewhere else was the look of pain and stress on almost every face. The bustling big city does its best to shape people in its own mold.

I believe that if Paul were speaking to us today, he would encourage us to put city life into perspective. So much of what people hurry to do each day is of only temporary value at best. The pursuit of money, the pursuit of things, the pursuit of earthly relationships— all of these can seem to be of the utmost importance at any given time, yet over the long term they fail to satisfy. Only eternal values can provide peace in the hustle and bustle of city life. Only a life that is grounded hour by hour and day by day in God's perspective on things can truly be a "quiet life." The city calls us to attend to our ways and our concerns, but our ways are not God's ways (see Isaiah 55:8, 9).

---

1. Quoted in Bill Hybels, *Christians in a Sex-Crazed Culture: A Frank Look at God's Good Gift* (Colorado Springs, Colo.: Chariot Victor Publishing, 1989), 17, 18.

The Dead in Christ
(1 Thessalonians 4:13-18)

When my mother died, we donated her body to medical science, according to her wishes. She died in full commitment to the Adventist faith regarding the state of the dead, the second coming of Jesus, and her ultimate resurrection. What happened to her while she was "sleeping" was of no concern to her, so she thought it no sacrilege to donate her body for research. Her future was firmly in God's hands, and He isn't indebted to preexisting matter to restore her consciousness at the resurrection. Her faith enabled her to face death confidently.

My family and I also comforted ourselves with these beliefs. These truths had an incredible impact on us. We figured that if the dead don't know anything, they aren't conscious of the passing of time. In terms of my mom's consciousness, then, it was as if she was already with Jesus. She had passed from suffering into unconscious death, and the next thing she would know, "in a moment, in the twinkling of an eye" (1 Corinthians 15:52, KJV), was that Jesus had returned to earth to take us all home. So we had no reason to mourn for her; she would be fine.

We held a memorial service for her about a month after her death, giving all who wanted to come the time to arrange to be there. The theme of the memorial was her life, not her death, and the theme text was Mark 14:8: "She did what she could" (NIV). Mother didn't have a high school education, she never preached a sermon, and she never gave a Bible study, but she had the gifts of hospitality and service. She used those gifts to influence deeply the lives of many people, including her children and grandchildren.

While we didn't intentionally exclude mourning from her funeral, there was none. The service was a celebration of her life and of the example that she set. Our hearts filled with joy as we remembered incidents in her life—some happy, some sad, some educational, and some that were downright hilarious!

At the memorial service, I shared my perception that my mother was an incredible combination of strength and permissiveness. She wasn't to be trifled with in matters of faith and health. She was an ever-present, "nagging" influence on behalf of truth and right. No one growing up in her home had any doubts as to what she believed or how she thought people ought to behave. At the same time, she allowed her children a lot of freedom to discover who they were and to make their own ways in life.

For instance, one Sabbath when I was nine years old, our church, which was located on the Upper East Side of Manhattan, had services planned for the whole afternoon and into the evening—services that my mother figured I wouldn't enjoy. A six-year-old girl whom my mother knew I rather liked was at the church that day too. Mother suggested that I walk this girl across Central Park to the Museum of Natural History and spend Sabbath afternoon enjoying the displays there, so that's what we did. Then, at five o'clock, I took the girl on the subway to her mother's home in New York City!

Speaking as someone who has raised children myself, I am in awe of the trust my mother bestowed on me, which she did frequently, not just this one time. While I never fully appreciated her "nagging," I determined early to never, ever disappoint her in the choices I made. By trusting us, she built a wall around my brother and me that prevented us from getting into smoking, drugs, alcohol, or crime!

The day of the memorial service I also told about my discovery that my health-reforming mother was human. One day when I was about six years old, she took me with her to the Port Authority Bus Terminal in New York City. We went there to meet someone who was coming from upstate New York to visit us. My mother and I watched bus after bus come and go from that place, but the person we were waiting for wasn't on any of them. Mom became increasingly agitated as time passed. When we had waited for a couple of hours to no avail, she took me by the arm and we marched to the convenience store in the center of the terminal. There she snapped up six Chunky bars (chocolate with raisins and nuts), gave me one to keep me quiet, and wolfed down the other five in a matter of minutes! She wasn't perfect, and she didn't claim to be perfect—most of the time.

The grandchildren weren't to be outdone. They told stories of how they had abused the freedom she gave them, playing hide and seek throughout her house in the middle of the night when she thought they were sleeping, sneaking gum and candy from her cupboards when she wasn't looking, and failing to clean up after themselves when she was tired. Yet they also said they had adopted her values and, in many ways, had become just like her! Her strength of character and personality combined with a trust that allowed a great deal of freedom created a legacy that lives on to this day.

The hundred people who attended her memorial service heard these and other stories and laughed so hard that their sides ached! That service was an amazing, comforting rite of passage. I doubt it could have been quite what it was had we not viewed death in the Adventist way, the way Paul lays out in the passage we'll look at in this chapter. While we sometimes take this passage for granted today, Paul wrote it to meet an emergency. Some very different kinds of funerals were being held in Thessalonica.

The Dead in Christ (1 Thessalonians 4:13-18)

The setting of 1 Thessalonians 4:13-18

In 1 Thessalonians 4:13–5:11, Paul continues the practical advice section of this letter. He writes a powerful description of the events surrounding the second coming of Jesus and the implications those events have for how Christians should behave. In verses 13–18, Paul reacts to some misunderstandings the Thessalonians had about what he taught while he was with them. They were distressed about what they thought would be the fate of believers who died before Jesus' return. Somehow they had come to believe that the people who will live until Jesus comes will gain some kind of advantage over those who have died before that event. Their confusion was understandable given how little time Paul had had to instruct them. They may have mixed what they remembered of Paul's teaching with ideas they brought with them from their Jewish or pagan backgrounds.

Within the thought world of Judaism in Paul's day, there were a variety of views regarding the events of the end time. At least one of these views may be relevant to our understanding of this passage: the belief that all of God's faithful would share in the new age that was coming, but that only those who were alive at the end would be carried up into heaven. Those who died before the end would be resurrected, but they would remain on earth. That meant, then, that those who died before the end were at a serious disadvantage. Not only would they miss out on the delights of heaven, but they would also be eternally separated from their loved ones who lived till the end.

It isn't surprising, then, that Paul began 1 Thessalonians 4:13–18 with a comment about the church's ignorance rather than what it already knew (cf. 1 Thessalonians 4:2; 5:2). On the topic of the Second Coming, there were things the church didn't know and there were things they would need to unlearn. The end result of their confusion was that their grief was no different from that of their pagan contemporaries. And that wasn't good—most pagans had no hope at all of life after death.

1 Thessalonians 4:13, 14

13But <u>we do not wish</u> you to be ignorant,
>   brothers,
>   about those who are asleep,
>   in order that you might not grieve
>   like others who have no hope.
14For if <u>we believe</u> that Jesus died and rose again,
>   so also (through Jesus?)
<u>God will bring</u> with Him
>   those who have fallen asleep
>   (through Jesus?).

In this letter, whenever Paul uses the term *brothers* he is introducing a new idea. Since he uses that word in 1 Thessalonians 4:13, we know he's introducing a new subject there. The point of concern is "those who are asleep." The present participle form in the original implies a present and ongoing state of "sleep" at the very time Paul is writing to the Thessalonian believers. We tend to use metaphors and analogies to describe the big issues of life because they help us describe and understand those issues. In the ancient world, sleep was a very common metaphor for death. The metaphor doesn't require the relative consciousness of actual sleep; most of the ancients didn't believe there was any kind of life or consciousness after death. So the issue before the Thessalonians was how to deal with the fact that some among them had died in the six months or so since Paul had left the community. For whatever reason, the church members were grieving those losses the way the pagans did.

So, Paul turns to end-time events in verse 14, not to establish all of the details of what will happen before the end, but to deal with a real-life situation current at that time. He writes this eschatology, then, on account of ethics. He means it to inform the church in Thessalonica how to behave in the face of death. This is evident in the clear statements he makes about his purpose. He says he's writing so that the Thessalonians might not grieve as do those who have no hope (verse 13). And he intends his theology to give them glorious reasons to comfort each other in times of loss (verse 18).

Verse 14 begins with the word *for,* indicating that its Paul's intention to focus on the problem stated in verse 13. In verse 14, Paul seeks to solve that problem by drawing a parallel between the death and resurrection of Jesus and the death and resurrection of the believer (see the parallel in the translation above). The resurrection of Jesus guarantees that all believers will also be resurrected at the Second Coming (see also 1 Corinthians 15:20–23). In other words, grieving over the death of believers as if there is no hope contradicts the testimony of Jesus' own death and resurrection. If Jesus was raised from the dead, those who believe in Him will also be raised. And if that's true, there is hope in the midst of grief. *Rom 6:3-11*

Before we move on to verse 15, we need to address the strange ways Paul has chosen to express what he's saying in verse 14—strange to us, at least! In this verse Paul said God will "bring with Him [Jesus]" those who have fallen asleep. Some read this as saying that those who have died in Jesus went to heaven at death and will return to this earth with Him when He comes from heaven. But this interpretation contradicts Paul's own teaching in verse 16 that the resurrection of dead believers occurs at the Second Coming, not before it.

The second difficulty is that the Greek original has Paul saying that the believers who have died have "fallen asleep *through* Jesus." The normal expression for a believer's death was "fallen asleep *in* Jesus" or "*in* Christ." A good example of this is the phrase the "dead *in* Christ" of verse 16. So what does falling asleep *through* Jesus mean?

There are two ways to understand Paul's use of "through Jesus" in verse 14. Some people say it is just another way of saying "in Christ," as in verse 16. In that case, these believers are simply being described as having died as Christians. But if that is the case, why Paul wrote "through" instead of "in" would still puzzle us.

The second suggestion, a more likely one, is that "through Jesus" should be connected to "God will bring" instead of "fallen asleep." (See the two possible placements listed with question marks in the translation on page 94. Word order isn't nearly as significant in Greek as it is in English.) If "through Jesus" belongs with "God will bring," then Paul is saying that Jesus is the Instrument through whom God will raise the dead at the end. God doesn't bring the resurrected Christians down to earth when Jesus comes, He brings them back up from the ground! In that case, "bring with Him" is simply the equivalent of the words *rose again* that Paul wrote earlier in the verse. Jesus' resurrection guarantees the resurrection of believers at His second coming.

While verse 14 comes across to us as being a little strange, Paul uses this language to address the hopeless grief of those who didn't grasp the full implications of Jesus' death. But Paul still hasn't dealt with the theological problem of where the resurrected believers go when Jesus comes. If our loved ones are raised from the dead but continue to be separated from us for eternity, what kind of hope is that? Paul addresses that aspect of Thessalonian belief in verses 15–18.

1 Thessalonians 4:15–18

[15]For <u>we say</u> this to you
>> by word of the Lord,
> that we who are alive,
>> who remain until the coming of the Lord,
> will not precede
>> those who have fallen asleep;
[16]because the Lord Himself
> will come down from heaven
>> with a cry of command,
>> with the voice of an archangel, and
>> with the trumpet call of God,
>> and the dead in Christ will rise first,
[17]then we who are alive,

who remain,
  will be carried up
    together
    with them
      in the clouds
        to meet the Lord
          in the air:
    and so we will always be
          with the Lord.
¹⁸For this reason, therefore,
    <u>encourage</u> one another
        with these words.

In 1 Thessalonians 4:13–5:11, Paul builds on the earthly teachings of Jesus. There are more than a dozen parallels between this end-time passage and the sayings of Jesus recorded in Matthew, Mark, and Luke. But when Paul talks about a word of the Lord in this passage, he is referring to something Jesus said that wasn't recorded in any of the Gospels, but which Paul has preserved for us.* Paul is probably not quoting Jesus directly here, but rather applying Jesus' words to the situation at hand.

This passage contains an interesting use of the word *loipos,* which is often translated as "remnant." In verse 13, I've translated it as "others," which is closer to what the word means in English. In that verse, the "others," the "remnant," are those outside the church. They have no hope. In verse 15, the "remnant" are believers who "remain" alive until Jesus comes. We can see, then, that the word can be used both positively and negatively.

The word *coming* in verse 15 is translated from the Greek word *parousia,* the most common term for the Second Coming. Paul is the first writer in the New Testament to use that term for the return of

---

* Acts 20:35 is a clearer example of such a saying.

Jesus, but he isn't the first to anticipate the return itself. The earliest Christians used the Aramaic term *maranatha,* which means "our Lord come." So teaching about the second coming of Jesus went back to the very beginnings of the Christian faith.

In this passage, Paul tells the Thessalonians that those who live until the coming of the Lord "will not precede" those who have fallen asleep (verse 15). What does that mean?

The best synonym for "to precede" is "to come before" or "to get ahead of." The Thessalonians' concern was that the believers who died before the Second Coming would somehow be disadvantaged throughout eternity as compared to the living. Paul's response focuses on the sequence of end-time events, the correct sequence resolving the Thessalonians' problem. Paul says the dead in Christ will rise first. Before the living will ascend to meet Jesus in the air (verse 17), before anything else happens, the righteous dead will be resurrected to join those who are still living on earth. In other words, the Thessalonian believers who died will be reunited with their loved ones even before any of them will meet Jesus. Those who have fallen asleep in Jesus are not disadvantaged at all. They "rise first." In other words, they're resurrected before anything else happens, so they will participate fully in the blessings of eternity.

The key theme of verse 17, then, may well be togetherness. The living and the dead are carried up together so they all can be together with the Lord. To always be with the Lord means no more waiting for Him and no more sleeping in Him. Neither group had been "with the Lord" in quite this sense before. The answer to hopeless grief is the hope of relationships that continue throughout all eternity.

Correcting misunderstandings

There are a couple of misunderstandings of Paul's meaning in 1 Thessalonians 4:15–18 that we should address. Some people claim verse 16 supports the idea of a rapture in which selected believers are snatched up from the earth secretly, leaving the rest of the world to wonder what happened. However, there's nothing about this verse that suggests secrecy. In fact, it pictures the very opposite. Paul says that the coming of the Lord is accompanied by "a cry of command, with the voice of an archangel, and with the trumpet call of God." The cry of command is apparently loud enough to penetrate graves and wake the righteous dead around the whole earth. It seems the voice of an archangel must also be a powerful instrument. In the Old Testament, the trumpet calls of God were associated with temple worship, battles, coronations, and God's appearance on Mount Sinai, all of which were public, noisy events. And in the New Testament, other than in Revelation, trumpets are almost always associated with the Second Coming itself. So this text offers no support for a *secret* rapture.

Another misunderstanding of Paul, sometimes based on 2 Corinthians 5, is the idea that believers go to heaven when they die. But this idea is completely incompatible with the scenario Paul pictures in 1 Thessalonians 4. First, he presents the model: Jesus rose from the dead and then He ascended to heaven; it wasn't the other way around. So it is with believers who die before Jesus' second coming. They will be raised from the dead, and then they will be carried up to heaven. It is only after this resurrection and ascension that the saints are "with the Lord." If believers went to heaven when they died, they wouldn't need to ascend at the Second Coming.

And there's more. If Paul taught the Thessalonians that the dead believers were already in heaven, why were they afraid they might "precede" them there? If the dead were already in heaven, why were the Thessalonians grieving like those who had no hope? If the problem was their ignorance of that "fact," why didn't Paul tell them, "Stop crying, they're already in Paradise"? Why did he comfort them by telling them that they will be reunited with those they have loved *when Jesus comes*? This passage makes it clear that Paul didn't believe that the saints go to heaven when they die.

This passage raises another issue—one that it doesn't fully settle. The issue is the question of where the saints go after they meet Jesus in the air. Many people think they meet Jesus in the air only to come back down to earth to reign with Him here for a thousand years—the millennium outlined in Revelation 20. But increasing numbers of scholars of all faiths are convinced otherwise. They note that the movement in 1 Thessalonians 4 is all upward; up from the ground in the resurrection and then up into the air to meet Jesus (verses 15–17). They note that Jesus Himself ascended to heaven after His resurrection, and Paul says the saints follow that model (verse 14). So the implication of our passage is that believers meet Jesus in the air so they can travel together with Him back to heaven.

The clearest indication of where believers go at the Second Coming, however, isn't in 1 Thessalonians 4 or Revelation 20. It's in verses 2 and 3 of John 14: "In my Father's house are many rooms; if it were not so, I would have told you. I am going there to prepare a place for you. And if I go and prepare a place for you, I will come back and take you to be with me that you also may be where I am" (NIV). Jesus doesn't tell His disciples, "I will come back [from heaven] so that where you are [on earth] I may be also." He tells them He is coming so that they, who have been on the earth, can be with Him in heaven. Jesus doesn't establish an earthly kingdom at His second coming; He takes the saints to be with Him in heaven, to live and reign there for the thousand years mentioned in Revelation 20.

In this passage, Paul met the Thessalonians where they were. I'm very grateful they had problems. If they hadn't, Paul might not have written these letters to them, and then my mom's funeral would have been very different.

CHAPTER 9

Final Events
(1 Thessalonians 5:1-11)

In chapter 4 of 1 Thessalonians, Paul began to address practical issues the Thessalonian church faced. First, he advised the Thessalonians with regard to issues of sexuality and employment (1 Thessalonians 4:1–12). Then he turned to the grief their erroneous beliefs about the Second Coming was causing the new believers, and he assuaged much of their grief by clarifying the order of events surrounding Jesus' return (verses 13–18).

In 1 Thessalonians 5:1–11, the Second Coming is still the primary theme, but the focus shifts. In this part of his letter, Paul isn't so much clarifying details about Jesus' return as he is proclaiming the need for constant readiness in light of the final judgment. The previous passage is encouraging; the end will be much more positive than the Thessalonians expected for the believers who have died before Jesus' return. But this passage focuses more on judgment. From this perspective, the condition of the Thessalonians was more serious than they realized.

The problem in the church seems to have been a theology of peace and safety combined, perhaps, with a bent toward calculating the timing of Jesus' return (sometimes called date setting). As a result, at least some of the Thessalonians were living without end-time urgency. In this chapter's passage, Paul offers a sharp critique of their approach to final events. His warnings are as relevant today as they were then.

Although Paul didn't use the word *judgment* in 1 Thessalonians 5:1–11, this passage is very much concerned with the issue of judgment. God's judgment isn't limited to something that happens in heaven at the end of time; it has real consequences for the life people live every day. Many people are uncomfortable with the theme of judgment. They don't like the negativity and threat that judgment brings to mind. But the biblical concept of judgment is broader than just threat, condemnation, and execution. It also has a positive side. Simple, everyday actions of mercy and kindness don't go unnoticed or unrewarded (e.g., see Matthew 10:42). Everything we do, whether positive or negative, is noticed and has meaning in the ultimate scheme of things.

The two-sided nature of judgment is evident in the earliest narratives of the Bible. In the Garden of Eden, God judges the sin of Adam and Eve negatively, but He judges Adam and Eve positively. He creates enmity between them and Satan, and, mercifully, He clothes them so they won't suffer unduly in the changing environment. In the fourth chapter of Genesis, God judges Cain negatively by sending him into exile. But Cain also receives a positive judgment. God places a mark on him so that no one will kill him. And in the Flood story, God judges the human race negatively in the destruction the Flood brings, but He also judges them positively by providing the ark as a way of escape. So, whenever God judges, there is both a positive and a negative side to that judgment.

The two sides of judgment are evidenced in 1 Thessalonians 5 by a series of contrasts such as darkness and light, night and day, and drunkenness and soberness.

1 Thessalonians 5:1–3

¹Now concerning the times and the seasons,

Final Events (1 Thessalonians 5:1-11)

brothers,
<u>you have no need</u> to be written to,
   ²for you yourselves accurately know
      that the Day of the Lord will come,
        like a thief in the night.
³When <u>they say,</u>
    "peace and safety,"
    then sudden destruction will come upon them,
    just like labor pains come upon a pregnant woman,
      and they will not escape.

These three verses tell us of the suddenness and unpredictability of the final events of earth's history. The words "now concerning" inform us that once again Paul is responding to questions and concerns from the congregation. He has shifted his thoughts from the order of events at the end to the "when" of the end. The use of the article *the* indicates that the phrase "*the* times and *the* seasons" is familiar to the church, as Paul himself notes, "You have no need to be written to, for you yourselves accurately know." The phrase "the times and the seasons" recalls Acts 1:6, 7, which says that right before the ascension Jesus' disciples asked Him about the timing of the final events of earth's history. Jesus replies that the times and seasons are God's concern, not theirs. So the phrase "the times and the seasons" has to do with attempts to calculate the timing of the end.

Paul's use of the phrase "peace and safety" here seems quite ironic. These nouns aren't paired together anywhere else in the Bible, but the phrase was a popular slogan when the Thessalonian letters were written. Around A.D. 50, the rulers of the Roman Empire had achieved what was called the *Pax Romana,* the Roman peace. No wars were being fought; no insurrections were being put down. Trade and travel flowed freely throughout the empire, aided by an amazing network of roads and the safety provided by the Roman authorities.

Many of the signs that Jesus said would come in the lifetime of the disciples weren't happening when Paul wrote. But Paul trusted the words of Jesus, and his trust was justified. About ten years later, the Roman peace broke down, and the troubles Jesus had predicted (Mark 13:5–23 and parallels) all began to take place.

The phrase "the Day of the Lord" is found in many Old Testament judgment passages. It identifies a decisive, end-time intervention by God, with a strong emphasis on the negative consequences of disobedience (Isaiah 13:6–9; Jeremiah 46:10; Ezekiel 30:2–12; Joel 1:14, 15; Amos 5:18–20; Obadiah 15; Zephaniah 1:11–18). In our current passage, Paul combines this earlier concept with the thief analogy that Jesus introduced (Matthew 24:43; Luke 12:39). The analogy of birth pains also recalls the teachings of Jesus on the Mount of Olives just before His crucifixion (Matthew 24:8; Mark 13:8).

The threefold combination of the Day of the Lord, a thief in the night, and the contractions that begin shortly before birth all illustrate the same point for Paul. For the wicked, the second coming of Jesus will be sudden, unexpected, and inescapable. The end time is not the time to prepare for the end. The time to prepare is now.

I find it interesting that Paul uses the analogy of birth contractions to describe the timing of the end. When a woman becomes pregnant, we know in general when the child is likely to arrive, but we can't be precise, at least with a natural birth. Similarly, while we can see that Jesus will come soon, we won't know the "day and hour" (Matthew 24:36, NKJV). The suddenness with which the end comes means there'll be no escape for the distracted or the complacent. The verses that follow, however, clearly say that those who watch need not fear the end.

1 Thessalonians 5:4, 5

⁴But <u>you</u>, brothers, <u>are</u> not in darkness,
    so that the Day overtakes you

like a thief.
⁵For <u>you are</u> all sons of light
 and sons of day.
<u>You are</u> not of night
 or of darkness.

In the opening verses of the fifth chapter of 1 Thessalonians, Paul addresses the condition of the unbelievers, not the believers. That is why he uses the third person to describe those who talk about peace and safety (verse 3). The Thessalonian church as a whole already knows that the Second Coming is certain, but its timing is a surprise. This surprise will be tragic for unbelievers because they will be completely unprepared for that event—some because they don't believe in the Second Coming, and others because they think they can delay their preparations until events convince them it is near.

Verse 3 contains a ruin-and-rescue contrast. Then, in verses 4 and 5, Paul switches from the third person to the second person. Addressing the church directly, he begins a series of contrasts, starting with day and night and darkness and light. In the Old Testament, light and darkness are quite commonly used as metaphors of spiritual life; they were popular in the Jewish world around the time of Jesus and Paul. While unbelievers will be surprised by the events of the end, believers won't be surprised. Why? Because they live in the light. Prophecy is not given to satisfy our curiosity about the future, but in His Word, God has given us enough information to enable us to be spiritually prepared for whatever lies ahead.

Preparation for the Second Coming means investing serious time in the Word of God. There are many distractions in today's world, from overwhelming jobs to e-mail to entertainment to a cornucopia of drugs and other mood enhancers. Paul's appeal comes down to us through the corridors of time. Set distractions aside. Give the Word of God the highest priority in your life, and you won't be caught off guard by events, no matter how surprising their timing may be.

1 Thessalonians 5:6–8

⁶So, therefore,
do not sleep,
    like the rest,
but be watchful and sober.
⁷For those who sleep, sleep at night, and
those who get drunk get drunk at night.
    ⁸But, being of day,
let us be sober,
    having put on a breastplate
      of faith
      and love,
    and a helmet,
      the hope of salvation.

Paul begins verse 6 with "so, therefore." He has established that true followers of Jesus are children of the light and of the day, so in verses 6–8 he builds on the metaphor of light and darkness in order to exhort the Thessalonians to continually improve their preparations for Jesus' return. While verse 7 offers a bit of a digression, verses 6 and 8 encourage the Thessalonians to be awake, sober, and armed for the challenges ahead.

The first contrast Paul uses is that of being asleep versus being awake. Since believers are children of the day, they shouldn't sleep "like the rest," another ironic use of the Greek word translated as "remnant." Here, sleep is a metaphor for spiritual laziness or lack of interest (cf. verse 10, where it's a metaphor for death). The expression "let us not sleep" might be translated better as "don't even start" (verse 6, NKJV). Paul assumes that they are already awake, but he encourages them to continually become more and more watchful.

Paul then changes the metaphor, encouraging the Thessalonians to be spiritually sober rather than drunk. In the ancient world, soberness was a symbol of philosophical reason. Paul wants the Thessalonians to be thoughtful and careful in their reasoning from Scripture. Many use the Bible for date setting and speculation. Paul wants believers to focus instead on the implications of Scripture for their own spiritual preparation. Those who are looking forward to the return of Jesus will be self-controlled in their relations to others, with emotions under the direction of Spirit-guided reason. They will work faithfully even when they don't feel like it, and they will restrain themselves sexually so that their feelings won't get in the way of fulfilling God's teachings in their lives.

Paul associates being awake and sober with daytime, and he says it is at night when people sleep and get drunk. Then, in verse 8, he switches abruptly to the imagery of a military guard. Guards need to be awake and sober at *all* times, day and night; so when it comes to watchfulness, they have to exceed the norm. Paul expects Christians also to exceed the norm in their preparations for the Second Coming. And like soldiers, Christians should put on all of their equipment before taking their posts.

Those who wrote the New Testament frequently used military analogies to teach about the spiritual life (see 2 Corinthians 10:3–5; Ephesians 6:10–17; Revelation 16:14–16). They didn't do so to promote physical combat; they were concerned with the battle for the mind. That's why Paul encouraged the Corinthians to "take captive every thought and make it obedient to Christ" (2 Corinthians 10:5, my translation).

Once again, Paul slips in the trio of faith, love, and hope, and once again hope is the last of the three he mentions. As in the opening verses of 1 Thessalonians, Paul uses hope last in order to underline his emphasis in this short book on the second coming of Jesus. And in 1 Thessalonians 5, he gives it even more emphasis than he does elsewhere, comparing hope alone to a piece of armor, whereas he has the breastplate represent both faith and love. Clearly, the military language of verse 8 is all about faith, love, and hope.

We usually use the word *salvation* to speak about acceptance of the gospel and the resulting life changes in the present. But in Paul's writings, salvation is a metaphor that almost always has to do with the future. In 1 Thessalonians 5, he speaks of the *hope* of salvation. He doesn't picture it as a present possession, but as something that believers will have at the end, when Jesus returns to save His people. Neither concept of salvation is wrong; salvation is a metaphor that can be used in more than one way.

In 1 Thessalonians 5:3–8, Paul draws a series of contrasts, some explicit and others in a more subtle fashion. I list them all below.

ruin/[rescue] (verse 3)
darkness/light (verses 4, 5)
night/day (verses 4, 5)
sleep/watch (verse 6)
drunk/sober (verses 6–8)
armed/[defenseless] (verse 8)
dressed/[naked] (verse 8)

1 Thessalonians 5:9–11

⁹Because <u>God did</u> not <u>appoint</u> us
   to wrath, but
   to the possession of salvation
      through our Lord Jesus Christ,
         ¹⁰*the One who died* for us,
            in order that,
               whether we are awake or asleep,
            we might live with Him.
¹¹Wherefore, <u>encourage</u> one another and
<u>build</u> each other <u>up,</u>
   just as you are, in fact, doing.

As we have seen, in 1 Thessalonians 5:1–8, Paul has drawn a series of contrasts to illustrate the two sides of judgment that will take place in connection with Jesus' second advent. In verses 9–11, Paul addresses the contrast between wrath and salvation.

Some people today feel that the biblical statements about God's wrath reflect the culture of Bible times more than the truth about God. It is true that there are human elements in the Bible, and it is also true that in the Bible God has accommodated His truth to the bounds of human understanding. But the concept of the wrath of God is not limited to the older parts of the Bible; it is widespread in the New Testament as well, coming from the lips of Jesus (Luke 21:23; see also John 3:36), the pen of Paul (Romans 1:18; 5:9; 1 Thessalonians 1:10), and the visions in Revelation (Revelation 6:16, 17; 15:1). So we cannot safely ignore the concept—it must express something very important about God and the plan of salvation. God's ways are not our ways (see Isaiah 55:8, 9).

While we can't go deeply into the matter here, we must be clear that the wrath of God spoken of in Scripture isn't irrational, impulsive rage. Instead, it's more like a nation's drive to bring to justice the lawbreakers who abuse and oppress other people. Since we have all broken the law of God, we would all be subject to the execution of justice were it not for the life, death, and resurrection of Jesus.

I'm reminded of the time when I was driving a little too fast on a rural road in upstate New York. My wife was in the front passenger seat of the car, and one of my church members was in the backseat— and she was telling me that her husband had just left her. The news was so distressing that I wasn't paying any attention at all to my speed. Sure enough, soon a big, red light was flashing behind me, suggesting that I was in trouble.

After a short conversation, the police officer handed me a traffic ticket that said, "The State of New York against Jon Paulien." What? Twenty million people in the state, and every one of them is mad at me? I know that idea is silly, but that's how I felt. I had violated the social order, and correction was needed. Similarly, the wrath of God is a metaphor telling us that we are out of order with the universe on account of our actions.

A few days later, I appeared before a judge in the small town where I was stopped. This judge was young and very kind. He asked me to tell my version of the story. I told him that I was a pastor and that the suffering of a member of my church who was in the backseat of my car had distracted me. He listened sympathetically, and graciously decided to waive the fine, saying he was assuming that I wouldn't be returning to his courtroom. Of course, I made sure I didn't end up there again!

The judge wasn't interesting in punishing me; he simply wanted me to change my behavior—and his grace was a stronger motivator for change than any fine would have been. That is like the good news about the wrath of God that shines through 1 Thessalonians 5:9–11. God isn't eager to pour out His wrath, or punitive justice, on us. He wants us to be saved, and, in Christ, He has provided all we need to avoid being destroyed in the judgment. That's why Paul thought that the wrath of God, rightly understood, was a reason for encouragement rather than fear (verse 11).

By means of all the contrasts in verses 4–9, Paul drew a sharp distinction between the lives and behaviors of the believers and those of outsiders. He didn't encourage the Thessalonian believers to be stressed about whether they were in or out. In the last days, believers can have confidence because in Christ there is assurance that they are children of the light—and encouragement is a much stronger motivation than is rebuke or compulsion.

Some people may wonder about all the metaphorical language in 1 Thessalonians. Isn't there anything in this letter that is literal and concrete?

Years ago, Ellen G. White wrote, "The Bible is written by inspired men, but it is not God's mode of thought and expression. It is that of humanity. God, as a writer, is not represented. Men will often say such an expression is not like God. But God has not put Himself in words, in logic, in rhetoric, on trial in the Bible."[1]

We need to keep in mind that when God communicates through

a prophet or an apostle, He meets people where they are. He uses illustrations from their cultures and settings, and He uses language that makes sense to them. That can make it harder for us—who live two thousand years later and in a very different culture—to figure out all that He's saying.

The Bible is clear enough that all can find their way to salvation, but it isn't so clear as to answer all of our questions about life, history, or science. God doesn't require us to know things He hasn't made clear. In eternity, everything will be made clear (1 Corinthians 13:12).

---

1. White, *Selected Messages,* 1:21.

CHAPTER

Church Life
(1 Thessalonians 5:12-28)

Paul concludes his first letter to the Thessalonians with a series of seventeen admonitions (1 Thessalonians 5:12–22) followed by a closing prayer (verses 23–28). The seventeen admonitions can be divided into two groups: counsels on ministry in the local church (verses 12–15), and counsels on general Christian experience (verses 16–22). The structure of the text identifies these two groups. The first nine begin with a verb and are ministry oriented. The last eight begin with words that in the original Greek feature the *p* sound, end with a verb, and are oriented to the believers' personal lives. These kinds of things are obvious in the original but are usually lost in translation.

In the concluding prayer, Paul summarizes a main theme of this letter: his wish that believers in Thessalonica and beyond would continue to grow in sanctification and holiness all the way up to the Second Coming itself. This growth is still crucial for congregations around the world today.

1 Thessalonians 5:12–15
¹²Now <u>we ask</u> you, brothers,
    to respect *those*

who labor among you, and
who are placed over you, and
who admonish you, [13]and
   to regard them super highly
      on account of their work.
<u>Be at peace</u> with one another.
[14]<u>We</u> also <u>encourage</u> you,
      brothers,
<u>admonish</u> the unruly,
<u>cheer up</u> the depressed,
<u>take an interest</u> in the weak,
<u>be patient</u> with everyone,
[15]<u>see that no one pays back</u> evil
   for anyone else's evil,
      but
always <u>pursue</u> what is good,
   toward one another and
   toward everyone.

Verses 12–15 follow naturally after the concluding admonition of the previous passage: "encourage one another and build each other up" (verse 11). This work takes place in congregations through mentoring and discipleship.

Most of verses 12 and 13 comprise a single sentence; "we ask you" is the main clause, and it is followed by a pair of infinitives: "to know/respect" and "to esteem/regard." The church is to respect and to have a high regard for its leaders. Paul identifies these leaders with a trio of participles that follows "respect"; they are "those who labor among you, who are placed over you, and who admonish you." These phrases don't imply three offices or classes of leaders. Rather, they reflect the kinds of things that church leaders do to mentor and grow the membership of the church in the things of the Lord.

At this time—around A.D. 50, roughly twenty years after the

crucifixion of Jesus—the church doesn't seem to have developed formal offices yet. Paul doesn't call the leaders of the church *elders* or *deacons*; he simply says, "Those . . . who are placed over you." Interestingly, the Greek word translated as "placed over you" (*proistēmi*) is the only leadership word the early church adopted from Greco-Roman government and social institutions. Christianity adopted the terms *elders, deacons,* and *overseers* later, drawing them from the Jewish synagogue and from roles related to home life.

Why did the early Christians use *proistēmi* while avoiding words such as "leader" (*hēgemon*), "ruler" (*archegos*), and "master" (*kurios*)? Probably because this word had the related meaning of "to have an interest in, show concern for, give aid." The verb form combines a sense of leadership and direction with a strong sense of caring concern. In the New Testament, terms such as "leader," "ruler," and "master" were reserved for Jesus Christ and for God, both of whom could be trusted with the kind of power and authority those words implied.

Why were the counsels in verses 12 and 13 needed? Given the unruly nature of the Thessalonian church, it is likely that some members were being disrespectful of authority. Paul's instruction that they were to "be at peace among yourselves" implies that there was a conflict in the church between the leaders and those being led (verse 13, NKJV). So Paul emphasized the importance of having a respectful attitude toward leadership—members should esteem their leaders highly on account of their work. This advice is particularly appropriate for members who are naturally combative or who are chronic complainers.

Can authority be abused? Do leaders sometimes lord it over members in ways that are destructive? Of course. Paul doesn't choose to address that distortion of leadership here, but he does so in 2 Corinthians 10–13, where he addresses a class of leaders that were undermining the gospel in their zeal for the letter of the law. Church life involves a constant tension between honoring those who lead in love and resisting those who use positions of authority to abuse others. The fact that some leaders abuse their authority isn't an excuse to disrespect all leaders as a matter of course. It is pride that leads us to think we understand the issues better than those who have been appointed to oversee things. We criticize from a distance, weighing every issue in light of what would be best for us personally and not with the wisdom that is needed to balance the whole. Balance is hard to maintain.

The word *admonish* in 1 Thessalonians 5:12 is interesting. It is a strong word that has the connotation of "instruct," "warn," or even "knock sense into." Paul acknowledges here that church leaders will often need to exercise tough love. This kind of leadership is not always welcome, so Paul goes on in verse 13 to ask the members to esteem their leaders highly on account of the difficult issues they have to deal with. Paul wants all the members of the church to be at peace with one other.

The language of these verses reflects ancient strategies for dealing with people. Thought leaders of Paul's day knew that dealing with people in a productive way requires great carefulness. They encouraged leaders to diagnose the condition of their followers carefully, to be sensitive to whether or not their followers were open to correction, to choose the right timing, and to apply the appropriate remedy. And above all else, Paul expected the leaders to examine themselves before they tried to correct others.

While much of what Paul says here about leadership would have been familiar to any Greek person of that time, Paul added two unique elements. First, God, as seen in Christ, provides the best Model of leadership—better than exemplified by any human being. And second, church leadership aims at a higher goal than creating good citizens; it aims to create a community that pleases God.

The task of Christian leaders

In verses 14 and 15, Paul turns his attention to the leaders of the church and how they should treat those under their care. He encourages the leaders in Thessalonica to "admonish the unruly" (verse 14, NASB). The Greek word underlying *unruly* implies people who purposely make themselves difficult to deal with. In 2 Thessalonians 3, the word is applied to those who were refusing to work. That would suggest the unruly were members who refused to support themselves. But the primary meaning of the word has more to do with an underlying disrespect for community rules than for behavior. When the actions of members show deliberate disrespect to church leaders or the wider community, those members are to be firmly confronted.

More positively, Paul instructs the leaders to "cheer up the depressed, take an interest in the weak, be patient with everyone" (1 Thessalonians 5:14). The word translated as "depressed" is a compound that could literally be translated as "little souls." These are people who have little self-confidence or sense of worth. They are anxious and worried about many things. Paul makes clear that depressed, anxious people matter to God. He says church leaders should encourage them even though doing so often consumes a great deal of time.

The word *weak* has to do primarily with physical limitations, but in the New Testament, it is usually used metaphorically for those with moral and spiritual limitations. The weak are gullible people, easily discouraged by hardship, and afraid of the unfamiliar. Their hearts are in the right place, but they lack knowledge and are often overwhelmed by life. They can survive only if they have help. Unfortunately, these people rarely attract help or ask for it, so Paul makes a special point of directing leaders to care for them whether or not they ask for help.

Finally, Paul directs church leaders to be patient with everyone. Since there are many different types of people, it is always helpful for leaders to know where people are coming from so they can fine-tune their responses to the specific conditions that generated the problem. They must be gentle with the weak and discouraged but must also knock sense into the unruly. And no matter who a leader is working with, patience is always a virtue.

Paul probably has leaders in mind in verse 15 also. In the original Greek, the concept of returning evil for evil is expressed in substitutionary language; Paul is speaking about people who do evil to retaliate for the evil done to them. When leaders are attacked by those who don't appreciate their admonitions, they may be tempted to use their positions to retaliate. But as Christ spelled out in Matthew 5:43–48, to retaliate would be to demonstrate that their leadership wasn't motivated by His spirit. To react to evil as Christ would is to bless rather than to curse and to show mercy rather than to retaliate. As applied to church leadership in verse 15, it means keeping oneself out of the way and keeping the good of others in mind in whatever actions one takes.

In all of this, we shouldn't forget verse 11: "Encourage one another and build each other up." Pastoral care often goes in both directions—each of us needs to be accountable to someone else, and we all need to be willing to hold others accountable. Sometimes the mentors need to be mentored, so, at those times, they must be willing to receive it. We need to learn both how to offer constructive criticism and how to accept it.

1 Thessalonians 5:16–22

[16]At all times <u>rejoice,</u>

[17]constantly <u>pray,</u>

[18]in all circumstances <u>give thanks,</u>
    for this is the will of God
        for you
            in Jesus Christ.

[19]The Spirit <u>do not quench,</u>

[20]prophecies <u>do not despise,</u>

[21]all things <u>test,</u>
the good <u>retain,</u>

[22]from every form of evil <u>abstain.</u>

In the above translation I retain the word order and flavor of the original, in which the verb comes at the end of the clauses. This series of brief commands contrasts sharply with the previous four verses (verses 12–15), where in each case the verb comes at the beginning of the phrase or sentence.

In verses 16–18, Paul addresses each member's personal relationship with God. He begins by telling us to be joyful "at all times" (verse 16). Paul used the same Greek word translated as "at all times" in 1 Thessalonians 1:2 with reference to his prayer life. Glenn Coon loved to say that there are ten times as many commands in the Bible to rejoice as there are commands to keep the Sabbath. We rarely give rejoicing the emphasis it deserves. A joyful life is one of the fruits of the Spirit (Galatians 5:22; see also Philippians 4:4), and we can have Spirit-filled joy even when we're suffering (1 Thessalonians 1:6). So, Christians never have an excuse for being completely without joy.

As we have seen, 1 Thessalonians is saturated in prayer. In chapter 5, verse 17, Paul encourages the readers of his letter to "constantly pray." Christ-filled music can help us to keep our minds focused on prayer. I find that at times when I'm really close to God yet not really thinking about anything particular at the moment, my mind defaults into Christian songs. One recent morning, as I lay in bed struggling to wake up, I realized that the song "Jesus Loves Me" was cycling through my head over and over again. That's much better than negative thinking!

I find support for this conclusion about the spiritual value of music in a statement Ellen G. White made in *The Desire of Ages* regarding the childhood behavior of Jesus.

[As a child,] Jesus carried into His labor cheerfulness and tact. It requires much patience and spirituality to bring Bible religion into the home life and into the workshop, to bear the strain of worldly business, and yet keep the eye single to the glory of God. . . . Often [Jesus] expressed the gladness of His heart by singing psalms and heavenly songs. Often the dwellers in Nazareth heard His voice raised in praise and thanksgiving to God. He held communion with heaven in song; and as His companions complained of weariness from labor, they were cheered by the sweet melody from His lips. His praise seemed to banish the evil angels, and, like incense, fill the place with fragrance.[1]

Thankfulness is another positive Christian attitude that Paul exhibited (1 Thessalonians 1:2; 2 Thessalonians 1:3). At the root of pagan depravity was a lack of gratitude to God (Romans 1:21). It is interesting to note, then, that the Greek words for "rejoice" and "be thankful" have the same basic root. The key to godly rejoicing is a continuing spirit of thankfulness to God. "Nothing tends more to promote health of body and of soul than does a spirit of gratitude and praise. It is a positive duty to resist melancholy, discontented thoughts and feelings—as much a duty as it is to pray."[2]

Putting 1 Thessalonians 5:16–18 in context presents an interesting challenge. Two questions confront us: First, in Paul's admonitions about joy and thankfulness in prayer, was he referring back to verses 12–15 and the issue of mentoring relationships in the church? In other words, is the root of our relationship with God the joy and gratitude we experience in prayer? Or, did Paul mean these lines to be connected with their attitude concerning prophecies (verses 19–22), which would point us to the conclusion that the main problem in Thessalonica was a lack of thankfulness for prophecies? You be the judge—but keep in mind that Paul may have placed these imperatives on prayer between mentoring and prophecy so they could shed light on both.

Paul begins the next section, verses 19–22, with a pair of negative commands that are continuous in emphasis. That means Paul was telling the Thessalonians to stop doing something they were doing on a regular basis. His words, translated from the Greek into a clear English paraphrase, admonish believers to "stop quenching the Spirit" and to "stop despising prophesyings" (verses 19, 20). When members of the church are setting dates for the Second Coming (verses 2, 3) and justifying spiritual and economic laziness (1 Thessalonians 4:10–12), it is understandable that other members might become skeptical of anything new, and particularly the claims of some that they have the gift of prophecy. But if we have "many lessons to learn, and many, many to unlearn,"[3] it is also spiritually dangerous for us to ignore everything that sounds new or different.

The focus of 1 Thessalonians 5:19–22 is on prophecies and prophetic activity, not prophets. In 1 Corinthians 14, Paul cautions the church not to be too accepting of claims that anyone, even a believer, has had a revelation from God. But here Paul warns about the other extreme. The church is to test such claims and "hold fast what is good" (1 Thessalonians 5:21, ESV), hold what is beneficial, in other words. In the context of a church, the great test of new light is whether it builds up the church or tears it apart.

One of the gifts of God to the church is the gift of discernment, which, in another of his letters, Paul listed right after the gift of prophecy (see 1 Corinthians 12:10). The believer who interprets or applies a prophecy rightly can be as important as the one who prophesies. There's wisdom in a saying attributed to Jesus, but not found in the New Testament: "Become like skillful money changers, who reject much of what they examine, but hold fast to whatever is genuine."[4] The gift of discernment is best exercised in a group in which people hold each other accountable—the kind of group Paul wrote of in verses 12–15.

People undermine the gift of prophecy in various ways. One of these is to quench the Spirit. We do this when we ignore or resist the work of a true prophet. If we refuse to examine how a revelation might apply to our lives, we have closed ourselves off from being taught by God. Another way we can undermine the gift of prophecy is to misinterpret or misapply what is said. We can approach a prophetic message with an open mind, but use it inappropriately by applying it to the immediate situation. A third way we can undermine the gift of prophecy is by attributing prophetic authority where God hasn't given it. The church must be continually vigilant, testing everything to see whether or not the prophecy builds up the church, whether or not the prophetic claim stands up to the tests God has given (see 1 Corinthians 14:4, 5, 29; Romans 12:2).

The church lives in the tension between revelation and reason, between openness to new light and the need to examine carefully all claims to truth. The church can't walk on solid ground without God's revelation, so it is dangerous to ignore prophetic messages. At the same time, however, accepting prophecies uncritically can be dangerous to the church (1 Thessalonians 5:2, 3). Reason applied in the context of a "multitude of counsellors" (Proverbs 11:14, KJV) is God's corrective to the natural human tendency to misapply His revelations.

1 Thessalonians 5:23–28

[23]May the God of peace Himself
sanctify you completely, and
may your whole spirit and
    soul and
    body
be preserved blamelessly
    at the coming
        of our Lord Jesus Christ.
[24]The One who calls you is faithful,
and He will do it.
[25]Brothers, pray for us.
[26]Greet all the brothers
    with a holy kiss.

²⁷I charge you
before the Lord
to have this letter read
by all the saints,
brothers.
²⁸The grace of our Lord Jesus Christ
be with you.

At the close of 1 Thessalonians, Paul returns to the language of prayer. His style in verses 23 and 24 is similar to that of chapter 3, verses 11–13. His main theme is also similar: being found blameless in holiness at the Second Coming. Paul makes a transition here from what the Thessalonians are supposed to do (1 Thessalonians 5:12–22) to what God does in us and for us: He sanctifies us, or makes us holy, and then comes to take us to live with Him (verses 23, 24).

Believers have often disagreed as to exactly what this passage text says about the nature of human beings and the kind of character we can expect to have when Jesus comes. In speaking of the "spirit and soul and body," Paul wasn't attempting to be scientific and precise about various layers of the human person. In biblical thought, mind and body are a unified whole, not parts that exist separately. So we shouldn't make too much of Paul's choice of words here. He was simply saying that every part of us is to be submitted to God. We're to give God full control of our thoughts, feelings, and actions.

The point in time Paul has in mind as he's praying is the moment of the Second Coming. Believers are to be "preserved" or "kept blameless" at or until the coming of the Lord. Paul isn't saying here that they must develop some higher form of character in the days before Jesus comes, but he *is* praying that the completeness of the dedication to God they already have will be guarded, protected, and maintained all the way to the end. So the word *sanctify* in this text may be closer to meaning something like "justify" than its normal meaning of character development. According to this letter, the

Thessalonians were far from perfect, but the spirituality they did have was worth preserving until Jesus comes.

We must view verse 23 in the light of verse 24. Our spiritual state is God's responsibility, not ours. The danger of striving for perfection is that we'll focus on ourselves, on what has been accomplished in us, and what remains to be done. Whatever level of perfection anyone reaches in this life is a miracle of God, not a result of human effort. When Paul writes about the call of God (verse 24), he uses a present participle—the form that emphasizes continuous action. The end-time work of sanctifying was a present reality among the Thessalonians and must be a present reality today as well.

Paul concludes the book with a stern warning, using special Greek language related to oaths (verses 25–28). Paul seems to have feared that some members of the church might keep his letter from the other members. Perhaps the unruly members tended to stay away from the church and needed to be invited to gather for the reading of the letter. Whatever the case, Paul charges those who receive the letter to read it to all the saints, whom he also calls brothers. In spite of the tensions in the church, Paul uses the term *brothers* two times in the conclusion of the book. The early Christians loved to speak of the church in terms of family, and they would greet one another with the kind of kiss that family members use to show their affection. Warts and all, the church is a family and needs to be treated as such.

---

1. White, *The Desire of Ages,* 73.

2. Ellen G. White, *The Ministry of Healing* (Mountain View, Calif.: Pacific Press®, 1942), 251.

3. Ellen G. White, "Search the Scriptures," *Advent Review and Sabbath Herald,* July 26, 1892.

4. Gerhard Kittel, ed., *Theological Dictionary of the New Testament,* vol. 2, trans. and ed. Geoffrey W. Bromiley (Grand Rapids, Mich.: Wm. B. Eerdmans, 1964), 375n21; author's translation.

Promise to the Persecuted
(2 Thessalonians 1:1-12)

A simple phone call could have cleared up a lot of the problems that Paul's churches faced, but, of course, there were no phones then, so believers had to track Paul down and hand-deliver a letter containing their questions. Then Paul would dictate a response and have it carried back to the church. The process might take months— months during which false doctrines and misunderstandings had time to develop and spread.

This seems to have happened in Thessalonica. In the time it took for Paul to gather information and write the response we know as 1 Thessalonians, new problems arose in the church. In addition, misunderstandings or misapplications of what Paul wrote in the first letter may have compounded these problems. Second Thessalonians is Paul's attempt to correct the situation.[1]

In the first chapter of 2 Thessalonians, Paul again looks forward to the outcome of his work for the Thessalonians. At the Second Coming, believers will be rescued from their persecutors by God's spectacular intervention in Christ. Second Thessalonians 1 provides additional information about the nature of the events that surround the return of Christ.

Promise to the Persecuted (2 Thessalonians 1:1-12)

2 Thessalonians 1:1, 2

¹Paul and

Silvanus and

Timothy

    to the church of the Thessalonians

        in God our Father and

        the Lord Jesus Christ.

²Grace to you and

peace

    from God our Father and

    the Lord Jesus Christ.

Paul had certain habitual ways of expressing things—including the style in which he greeted people in his letters. The opening of 2 Thessalonians is almost identical to the opening of 1 Thessalonians. In today's world, we might suspect that Paul was using a computer macro, which would start every letter with the same basic introduction. However, there is one difference between 1 and 2 Thessalonians—a difference all the Greek manuscripts have preserved. Paul changes the introduction from "in God the Father" (1 Thessalonians 1:1) to "in God *our* Father" (2 Thessalonians 1:1; emphasis added). This change adds a relational touch. There are people who feel close to Jesus, yet who are afraid of God the Father. Paul assures the Thessalonians that they can have as much confidence in their relationship with the Father as they do with the Son. Jesus came to this earth to show us what the Father is like. That point is made most powerfully in the prologue to the fourth Gospel (John 1:1–18).

2 Thessalonians 1:3–10

³<u>We are obligated</u> to give thanks to God

    always for you,

  brothers,

as is right,
because your faith is growing abundantly,
and the love of every one of you
     for each other
  is increasing,
⁴so that we ourselves boast about you
     among the churches of God
  because of your patience
  and faith
     in all your persecutions and
     in the afflictions
       you are enduring,
⁵the evidence of the righteous judgment of God,
     so that you might be made worthy
       of the kingdom of God,
       for which you are suffering,
⁶since it is indeed just
     in God's mind
   to repay with affliction
       those who are afflicting you,
⁷and rest to you
       who are afflicted
         along with us,
       at the revelation of the Lord Jesus
       from heaven
       with His mighty angels
       ⁸in flaming fire,
   directing vengeance
       toward those who don't know God,
       and who do not obey the gospel
         of our Lord Jesus Christ,
       ⁹who pay the penalty
         of eternal destruction,

away from the face of the Lord
and from the glory of His power,
¹⁰on that day when He comes
to be glorified in all His saints,
and to be marveled at in all who believe,
because our witness was believed by you.

This is a hefty piece of text for us to consider. I would have broken it up into smaller pieces, but the whole eight-verse passage is a single sentence in the Greek. In English, the King James translation is punctuated to reflect this. While the sentence as a whole focuses primarily on events surrounding the second coming of Jesus, the main clause of the sentence is, "We are obligated to give thanks to God always for you" (verse 3). Paul's comments on the return of Jesus (verses 6–10) are part of the reason he thanks God concerning them.

Now that you've seen the flow of the whole sentence, with all of its subordinate clauses (I have tried to retain the flavor of the Greek grammar), let's repeat the first two verses of this section (verses 3, 4) so we can focus more directly on the details of the text.

2 Thessalonians 1:3, 4

³We are obligated to give thanks to God
always for you,
brothers,
as is right,
because your faith is growing abundantly,
and the love of every one of you
for each other
is increasing,
⁴so that we ourselves boast about you
among the churches of God
because of your patience

and faith
in all your persecutions and
in the afflictions
you are enduring

Once again we are in the realm of prayer, a place Paul seems to visit frequently in these letters. Paul feels obligated to thank God for the Thessalonians for two reasons: first, because their faith is "super-growing" (one of Paul's many compound "super" words). There was a time when Paul worried about the faith of the Thessalonians (1 Thessalonians 3:1–10), but that is no longer the case. Their faith was "growing abundantly." Paul thanks God because the Thessalonians' love for one another is also increasing. In the original Greek, both verbs ("is growing" and "is increasing") are in the present tense. This means that the Thessalonians were consistently and steadily growing in faith and increasing in love. This kind of growth is basic to any healthy church. Plants that don't grow will die. So will churches that don't grow spiritually.

Paul affirms the Thessalonian believers in part because they are continuing to suffer persecution. Paul boasts about their patience in affliction. The Thessalonians have become models of Christian commitment under fire, either because their persecution was more severe than most, or because the way that they responded to it was unique among the churches Paul worked with (see 1 Thessalonians 1:6, 7).

My own experience has taught me that character growth happens best in an atmosphere of grace and acceptance. I grew up in a good Adventist home, but I tended to do right out of fear of God's punishment rather than out of a clear sense that God loved and accepted me. No matter how hard I tried, I seemed to make the same mistakes over and over again. But when I began to truly believe that God accepted me, I began to experience spiritual growth spontaneously.

By beholding we are changed. If we think God is stern and vengeful, we will tend to become stern and vengeful ourselves. But if we think God is gracious and accepting, we will tend to take on those characteristics. When one looks at Jesus, it is not hard to see which picture of God is more accurate.

2 Thessalonians 1:5, 6
⁵the evidence of the righteous judgment of God,
   so that you might be made worthy
     of the kingdom of God,
      for which you are suffering,
⁶since it is indeed just
   in God's mind
     to repay with affliction
      those who are afflicting you

The word *evidence* at the beginning of verse 5 means the proof or the plain indication of something. It refers back to something in verse 4, but what? Is it the apostle's boasting that is evidence of "the righteous judgment of God"? Or is it the church's patience and faith? Or, perhaps, the kind of persecution they were enduring? The phrase that's closest to the word *evidence* would normally be the one referred to. But what does the persecution of Christians prove about the righteous judgment of God? The evidence Paul is writing about is certainly not evidence of God's judgment *against* His people. To the contrary, it is a pointer to the future judgment, in which the people of God are vindicated and those who persecuted them are paid back in kind. (We'll see that later in this chapter.)

There's a message for us here. God's judgment will set things right. Those who persecute the people of God will one day face His justice, and those who experience injustice today on account of their faith can look to God's judgment with confidence. When it takes place, it will be evident that they were the objects of God's favor all along.

The New Testament encourages believers to exhibit grace, mercy, and forgiveness toward others. But when these actions are met with

129

curses, blows, and confinement, it is encouraging to know that injustice will not last forever. So, Paul invites the saints of God to be patient (2 Thessalonians 1:3, 4; see also Revelation 14:12). Their patience and faith as they endure trials not only make life more bearable, but they also reveal that God has chosen them. Consequently, suffering for one's faith can be a reason for rejoicing (1 Thessalonians 1:6, 7). It is real-life evidence of whose side we will be on when Jesus comes.

In verse 5, the righteous judgment of God is seen in His approval of the Thessalonians. In verse 6, it is seen in the condemnation and destruction of their persecutors. In both cases, the judgment is the end-time outcome of present conduct.

2 Thessalonians 1:7–9

⁷and rest to you
    who are afflicted
      along with us,
  at the revelation of the Lord Jesus
    from heaven
    with His mighty angels
    ⁸in flaming fire,
directing vengeance
    toward those who don't know God,
    and who do not obey the gospel
      of our Lord Jesus Christ,
  ⁹who pay the penalty
    of eternal destruction,
    away from the face of the Lord
    and from the glory of His power

In today's world, many people are uncomfortable with the language of this text. They feel that a God of love, grace, and mercy would have nothing to do with "pay back," vengeance, punishment, and the infliction of suffering (verse 6, NIV). They believe that talk about violence increases violence.

How shall we view these passages? Is God vengeful?

First, we must read passages like this one in 2 Thessalonians with the larger context of the Bible in mind—specifically, its message that God loves all people and that He doesn't want anyone to die.

Second, while the thoughts of those who wrote the Bible were inspired by the Holy Spirit, it was the human writers who chose the words they used. As we have noted previously, Ellen G. White pointed to this fact.[2] To some degree, then, the violent language of the Bible may be an accommodation to human need.

Third, we must take into account the fact that metaphors are used freely in the Bible, and the men who wrote the Bible chose them to communicate to people living in particular times and places.

Fourth, any good government in today's world must at some point exercise violence in order to restrain evil. Governmental violence is not always graphic and bloody, of course. It may merely involve the kind of restraint exercised when a policeman pulls a person over in a speed trap or when an agent of the government audits a person's taxes.

You don't consider that violence? How fast would you drive if there were no police? How much would you pay the government if taxes were voluntary? How eager are most convicts to stay in jail? Good governments provide the restraint that's needed so that we can live together in peace.

When dealing with an Adolf Hitler or a Saddam Hussein, violence necessarily becomes more brutal. Evil never gives way voluntarily. And the greater the power and brutality of evil, the greater the force needed to undo that evil. The images in this passage are not pretty, but they assure us that God will do whatever it takes to end violence and oppression (see Revelation 16:4–7). While God's violence is necessary, it is overseen and limited by Jesus, the merciful Savior. Jesus understands the cost of suffering because He has experienced it. We can trust Him to exercise divine justice without going into overkill. The wicked *will* suffer, but not one iota more than necessary.

However, Paul's goal in this passage wasn't to rejoice in vengeance but to encourage the abused and oppressed: The day of justice is coming, so we don't need to take justice into our own hands. A righteous God who measures justice with care will judge on our behalf. The core of this judgment is actually the other side of 1 Thessalonians 4. That passage says the Second Coming will enable the Thessalonians to be with the Lord. This passage indicates that the Second Coming will drive those who were persecuting the Thessalonians away from the face of the Lord—not because He hates them, but because the evil in their characters make them unable to handle the glorious presence of God.

2 Thessalonians 1:10

[10]on that day when He comes
    to be glorified in all His saints,
    and to be marveled at in all who believe,
        because our witness was believed by you.

Second Thessalonians 1:3–10, the full sentence, provides a number of important details about the second coming of Jesus. When Jesus returns, He will afflict the afflicters and give the afflicted rest (see verses 6, 7, ESV). He will come down from heaven in the company of powerful angels (verse 7). He will come with flaming fire and execute justice on those who have rejected God and the gospel of Jesus Christ (verse 8). The wicked will be destroyed at His coming (verses 8, 9), and the righteous will bring glory to Christ (verse 10). I have placed verse 10 all by itself because in it Paul transitions from the judgment of the wicked to the experience of the righteous.

Some members of the church in Thessalonica had taken up the idea that the Day of the Lord had already come (see 2 Thessalonians 2:1–3 and the next chapter of this book). Paul wrote these opening

lines with them in mind. He was saying that the idea that the Day of
the Lord was already in the past didn't fit the evidence. It was as if
Paul were saying, Has God been fully glorified on the earth? (Definitely not.) Have the wicked already been destroyed by fire? (No, they
are still persecuting believers.) The vividness of Paul's account of the
Second Coming was proof positive that the end had not already come.

2 Thessalonians 1:11, 12

[11]With this end in view
   we pray always for you,
      in order that our God might make you
         worthy of this calling,
      and He might fill up
         (your) every intention of goodness
         and work of faith
         with power,
      [12]so that the name of our Lord Jesus
         might be glorified in you all,
         and you in Him,
            according to the grace
               of our God and
               the Lord Jesus Christ.

Verse 11 makes it clear that character matters. After all, character
is the one thing that we all take with us into eternity.[3] Paul prays that
God will make each of the Thessalonians worthy to participate on
the day when Jesus returns. Paul knows their good intentions and
working faith, and he prays that God will supply that which they
cannot do; that He will give them whatever they need to become
what He wants them to be. As in 1 Thessalonians 5:24, this is not a
call for the Thessalonian believers to expend extra effort, but a call
for them to continually place themselves in the hands of God so He
can mold and shape their characters. In the end, character is made

up of small choices made on a daily basis. When we choose to place ourselves and our characters in God's hands moment by moment, He will do what it takes to make us worthy to glorify Him at His return. This growth in character is never the ground of our salvation; rather, it is the fruit of a saving relationship with Jesus Christ.

In verse 12, Paul shifts easily from God to Jesus, using the two terms interchangeably. While the Thessalonian letters are among the earliest writings of the New Testament, it is clear that Paul's concept of monotheism—his belief that there is only one God—includes Jesus. The Son isn't some secondary god or minor deity; He is fully equal to the Father. This teaching is very important to us. The greater Jesus is, the more powerful is His salvation, and the clearer the picture of God we receive as we contemplate Jesus' life, death, resurrection, and return. If Jesus is fully included in the Jewish concept of one God, then He is the clearest revelation of what God is like in a form that humans could see, handle, and begin to understand.

The faith shown by an Adventist farmer revealed that he understood the implications of what I've written about in this chapter. One Friday just before harvest was to begin, the news spread that that a massive swarm of locusts was heading toward the region where he lived. The neighboring farmers hurriedly prepared to work all Friday night and all day Saturday to harvest their crops before the locusts arrived, but the Adventist farmer prepared for the Sabbath as usual. His neighbors tried to persuade him to work on "his" Sabbath just this once. They cared about him and didn't want to see him or his family hurt. But the Adventist farmer was resolute. He would obey the commandment and leave his farm in God's hands.

On Sunday morning, the Adventist farmer woke up and looked out the window to see what had happened. Unfortunately, while all the other farmers had saved their crops, his were completely gone. The locusts had eaten every bit.

That morning the other farmers dropped by the Adventist farmer's place on their way to church. "What happened?" they asked. "Why didn't God protect your harvest when you were so faithful to what you believe?"

The farmer's answer was short and to the point of 2 Thessalonians 1: "God doesn't always make a final settlement in October."

---

1. Based on the introductory notes to 2 Thessalonians in the *NKJV Study Bible* (Nashville: Thomas Nelson Publishers, 1997), 2031.

2. White, *Selected Messages,* 1:21.

3. See Ellen G. White, *Christ's Object Lessons* (Mountain View, Calif.: Pacific Press®, 1941), 342, 361; Ellen G. White, *Education* (Mountain View, Calif.: Pacific Press®, 1952), 307.

The Antichrist
(2 Thessalonians 2:1-12)

In chapters 4 and 5 of 1 Thessalonians, Paul wrote about the end time, beginning with words of encouragement to the Thessalonian believers (1 Thessalonians 4:13–18) and then moving on to exhortation (1 Thessalonians 5:1–11). Paul followed the same pattern in his second letter. He first sought to encourage the Thessalonians in the midst of their afflictions (2 Thessalonians 1:1–12) and then he corrected their concept of the future (2 Thessalonians 2:1–12).

In the passage we'll consider in this chapter, Paul minimizes the apocalyptic details. He told the Thessalonians the details while he was with them (verse 5), so he doesn't need to lay them out again. Instead, his goal is pastoral; he means to calm the Thessalonian believers and to persuade them to be more patient as they watch and wait for the end time. In view of his rather limited objectives, he doesn't answer many of the questions we would like to see him address. In fact, this passage is one of the most difficult to understand in all of the New Testament, as we will see.

2 Thessalonians 2:1–3a

¹Now,

    with reference to the coming

of our Lord Jesus Christ
and our gathering
to Him,
<u>we implore</u> you, brothers,
[2]that you might not be quickly shaken
from your mind,
or disturbed,
either by a spirit,
or a word,
or a letter,
as it were from us,
implying that the Day of the Lord has already come.
[3a]<u>Do not let</u> anyone deceive you
in any way.

In the original Greek, several of the words and phrases in this passage bear similarities to 1 Thessalonians 4:13–5:11, among them the "coming of the Lord" (1 Thessalonians 4:15), the gathering (1 Thessalonians 4:17), and the Day of the Lord (1 Thessalonians 5:2). So, Paul feels the need to clarify not only what he said about the end time when he was there in person, but also what he said about it in his first letter to the Thessalonians.

The vocabulary—"unsettled," "alarmed," and "deceive[d]"—also reminds us of the teachings of Jesus (2 Thessalonians 2:2, 3, NIV). In fact, the Greek word translated as "alarmed" here, *throeō,* is used only two other times in the New Testament, both of them in Jesus' sermon about the end time: Matthew 24:6 and Mark 13:7. Apparently, some Christians in Thessalonica had failed to heed Jesus' instruction to avoid becoming overly excited about current events. Wars, rumors of wars, famines, earthquakes, and epidemics grab our attention, but they don't tell us how much time is left on the prophetic clock. Events of this nature are to be expected in a sin-cursed world.

Paul doesn't seem to be sure exactly what has gone wrong in the Thessalonian church, but he envisions three possible sources of confusion. The first one he lists is "a spirit" (2 Thessalonians 2:2). Here, he is likely referring to a faulty prophetic teaching—either that of a false prophet or something that has grown out of a misunderstanding of Paul's first letter. The second possible source is the spoken word—a teaching passed by word of mouth from member to member. And the third one Paul lists is a letter "supposed to have come from us" (verse 2, NIV). Here he is referring either to a letter forged in his name or to a misuse of one of his genuine letters.

No matter how carefully a pastor may watch over a church, there are multiple ways in which false ideas can take root. It is sometimes easier for members to accept a report or rumor than to examine the Scriptures for themselves. Sometimes the new ideas may even be biblical—the fault being someone's emphasizing them to the neglect of complementary teachings that would provide balance.

The latter seems to have been the problem in Thessalonica. The Thessalonians knew a lot about the second coming of Jesus and the events preceding His return, but they tended to emphasize one extreme or another of the teaching without the counterbalancing perspectives. At first, they lamented the delay in Jesus' return (1 Thessalonians 4:13–15). Now they seem to have drawn the conclusion that they were already in the midst of the final events. Paul responds to the problem with a very complex sentence.

2 Thessalonians 2:3b–4

3bBecause [that Day will not come]
    except the apostasy comes first,
       even the revelation of the man of lawlessness,
         the son of destruction,
         4who opposes
         or exalts himself
            over everything that is called God

> or is an object of worship,
> so as to sit in the temple of God
>   as God,
>   proclaiming himself to be God.

The words in brackets, "that Day will not come," aren't actually in verse 3. I've put them there because this sentence of Paul's—verses 3 and 4—is not only complex, it is also incomplete. I've added the subject and the verb because the sentence can't be understood without them.

Paul states that the Day of the Lord will not come until certain events have taken place. There is to be a rebellion or apostasy (Greek: *apostasia*) before the end, during which the identity of a "man of sin" or a "man of lawlessness" becomes public knowledge.* Paul elaborates on that revelation in verses 8–10, where he says it is due to the working of Satan just before Jesus comes.

Jesus noted that there would be an increase of lawlessness as the end approaches (Matthew 24:12). But He emphasized the mighty crescendo of the gospel as it is preached to the whole world just before the end (verse 14). Paul, in contrast, focused primarily on the growing tide of evil marked by the exposure of the lawless one before the end (2 Thessalonians 2:3, 4, 8–12). The two ideas aren't contradictory; they are complementary perspectives of the same basic event. First Timothy 4:1–5 and 2 Timothy 3:1–5 spell out in further detail the kinds of things that will characterize this apostasy.

Who is this man of sin or lawlessness? Paul doesn't identify him specifically, but a number of the characteristics listed in verse 4 point toward Satan himself. The lawless one is an opposer or adversary (Zechariah 3:1, 2; 1 Timothy 5:14, 15); an "accuser of our brethren" (Revelation 12:10, NKJV). He claims to be God and seeks to take God's place on God's throne (Isaiah 14; Ezekiel 28). All of these texts

---

* The words sound similar in the Greek, and thus the scribes taking dictation sometimes switched them.

use language like that of Paul in 2 Thessalonians to refer to the activity of Satan on this earth, though sometimes this activity was carried out through representatives like the kings of Tyre and Babylon.

On the other hand, the language of 2 Thessalonians 2:4 also recalls such passages as Daniel 8:9–12, 23–25, and 11:31–39, where the little-horn power is portrayed in terms that are more human than supernatural. Like the little horn, Paul's lawless one seeks to dominate the temple of God—terminology that in Paul's writings usually means the church, the center of spiritual authority on earth (1 Corinthians 3:16, 17; 2 Corinthians 6:16). So the description in 2 Thessalonians 2:4 could just as well apply to a human representative of Satan as to Satan himself.

Whoever this man of lawlessness is, the consistent use of the present tense in the original demonstrates that Paul considered him to be at work already (verses 4, 7).* In Greek, the present tense emphasizes ongoing activity—in this case, of the lawless one. The lawless one continually opposes, continually exalts himself, continually claims to be God, and continually tries to seat himself upon the throne in God's temple. Paul doesn't limit the lawless one to a particular point in time. He is either Satan himself or a series of human agents operating on Satan's behalf. We can't fully determine the identity of the lawless one from verses 3 and 4 alone.

After a brief digression in verse 5, Paul introduces another character in the end-time drama—a restraining force or person who prevents the lawless one from being revealed.

2 Thessalonians 2:5–7

⁵Don't you remember

---

* Bible translations that use the word *will*—for example, in "will oppose and will exalt himself" (2 Thessalonians 2:4, NIV)—suggest that in Paul's day, the workings of the lawless one were still future. But in the Greek, these verbs are in the present tense, not the future tense. So, the addition of the word *will* is an interpretation made by the translator—one that isn't supported by the text.

that when I was with you
    I told you these things?
⁶And now <u>you know</u> what is restraining him,
    in order that he might be revealed
      in his own time.
⁷For <u>the mystery</u> of lawlessness <u>is</u> already at work,
  only <u>he who </u>now <u>restrains [will continue]</u>
    until he is out of the way.

Once again we wish we knew what Paul had told the Thessalonians previously. He tells us even less about the restrainer than he does about the man of lawlessness, and there are a number of other uncertainties in these verses as well. In verse 6, "what is restraining" is in the neuter gender, implying that it is a thing; but in verse 7, "he who now restrains" is in the masculine gender, implying that it is a person. Similarly, in verse 7, the "mystery of lawlessness" is in the neuter gender, but "the lawless one" is masculine in verse 8.

In addition to these puzzlers, verse 7 isn't clear about whether the restraining power is taken out of the way by a greater power or whether it/he has the authority to remove himself. The Greek word translated as "is" at the end of verse 7 ("*is* out of the way") is a Greek deponent, which means it is middle or passive in form but usually active in meaning. So translations such as the King James Version and the New International Version ("*taken* out of the way") imply more than the language of the text actually states. We don't know from the text itself if the restrainer operates completely on his own (as would God or the Holy Spirit) or if it is some subordinate power (such as Satan or the Roman Empire).

Whoever the restrainer is, he was already functioning in Paul's day. This is clear from the present tenses (verse 6, "is restraining"; verse 7, "is already at work") and the explicit "he who *now* restrains" (verse 7; emphasis added). Because of the restrainer, the lawlessness at work in Paul's day and beyond is promoted by a mystery, a secret power that has not yet been fully revealed to the public. The restrainer is a power that upholds the law (restrains lawlessness), and is on a mission that has time factors set by God. (He continues his work until an appointed time, verse 7.)

In a sense, by holding back the revelation of lawlessness, the restrainer is holding back the end itself. In writing of the restrainer, Paul uses both personal and impersonal terms. The Thessalonians know "*what* is holding him back" (verse 6, NIV; emphasis added) and "*who* now restrains" (verse 7; emphasis added). So, the restrainer is more than a person; the restrainer is also a power.* Not only is the restrainer powerful enough to prevent the revelation of Satan and his agent (verses 3, 4, 9), he (it?) appears to continue to function until just before the end itself (verse 8), while the lawless one is destroyed almost as soon as he appears.

When we combine the information contained in verses 3 through 7, we can see that Paul's outline of the future that extended from his time to the end has three stages. The third stage is the Second Coming, which is mentioned briefly in verse 8. The revelation of the man of sin (verse 3), the lawless one (verse 8), takes place before that final stage. That revelation is described in verses 8–12. And the stage that begins all the way back in Paul's day is characterized as a time of mystery and restraint (verses 6, 7).

Who is the restrainer, and what power or force does he use to restrain? There are two options that fit this passage fairly well. First, the restrainer could be the Roman emperor and/or the Roman Empire of Paul's day. The empire was constantly restraining forces that otherwise would have hindered Paul's ministry. The collapse of the empire opened the way for the medieval papacy. But the lack of a true passive, indicating the removal of the restrainer by a higher power, suggests that the restrainer is considerably more powerful than the Roman Empire. After all, the Roman Empire wasn't pow-

---

* As is the lawless one, compare verses 3 and 7.

erful enough on its own to restrain Satan and the earthly powers subordinate to him.

I'm not saying that Paul couldn't have had this option in mind. In its favor is the fact that many of the early church fathers—church leaders of the second through the fourth centuries—believed that the fall of the Roman Empire would usher in the antichrist and the events of the end. But the wording of the Greek version of verses 4–7 is too ambiguous to compel us to settle on this conclusion.

A second major possibility is that the restrainer is much more powerful and positive than the Roman Empire. In much of the New Testament, the events leading up to the Second Coming are precipitated, not by political events like the fall of the Roman Empire, but by the final proclamation of the gospel (Matthew 24:14; Mark 13:10; Revelation 14:6, 7). If this was Paul's meaning here, he would be underlining a point that Jesus and John the revelator also made: the everlasting gospel will be taken to the whole world and then the end will come. In this case, God Himself would be the Restrainer—the One who holds back the final events until everyone has heard the gospel.

There may be a third option. Paul may have deliberately used ambiguous language to allow readers down through the ages to see his words here as applying to God's work in their own time and place, without closing the door to an even more powerful work of God at the very end. Second Thessalonians 2:10b–12 hints at how Paul might have responded to this suggestion, but before we go there, we need to see the outcome of the revelation of the man of sin, the lawless one.

2 Thessalonians 2:8–10a

⁸And then <u>the lawless one will be revealed,</u>
    whom the Lord Jesus will overthrow
      by the breath of His mouth,
    and bring an end to

by the brightness of His coming,
[9]whose coming is according to the working of Satan
in all kinds of miracles
and signs
and lying wonders
[10a]and in every deception of unrighteousness
among those who are being destroyed.

Paul introduced the man of sin, the lawless one, in 2 Thessalonians 2:3, 4. Through much of Christian history this person or power has operated behind the scenes, attempting to undermine God's law, particularly the Sabbath, and to usurp powers that belong only to Christ. Passages such as Daniel 7:20–25 (the little horn) and Revelation 13:1–7 (the beast from the sea) indicate that this same power operated after the fall of the Roman Empire, combining both religious and secular authority to persecute the saints of God. The only power that fits all the specifications of these prophecies is the medieval papacy. Students of the Bible from the Middle Ages through to our day have identified this institution as the antichrist, and it does fit the specification of 2 Thessalonians 2 that the man of sin or lawlessness would be both masculine (a person) and neuter (a power or institution).

In verse 7, the term *mystery of lawlessness* appropriately describes the activity of this power up till now. But at the close of history, just before the Second Coming, there will be an even more universal and blatant defiance of God and His laws. The continuity of the powers spoken of both in 2 Thessalonians 2 and elsewhere (Daniel 7 and Revelation 13) indicates that the papacy will play a major role at the end of time as well.

However, 2 Thessalonians 2:8–10a draws back the curtain to reveal an even greater antichrist behind the one that has operated among the nations through most of the past two millenniums. Satan himself is the author and finisher of the deceptions of the end time.

The Antichrist (2 Thessalonians 2:1-12)

As the time of Jesus' return approaches, events will force Satan into making a final act of desperation. He will throw caution to the wind and appear in person to mimic the earthly ministry of Jesus. (Compare the language of verse 9 with Acts 2:22.) Through counterfeit miracles, he will attempt to draw people's attention away from the gospel (the life, death, and resurrection of Jesus) and even from the Second Coming itself. But his desperate action will fail. His henchmen will be destroyed at Jesus' return; and for a thousand years, Satan will be left to ponder the mess that sin has made of this world.

2 Thessalonians 2:10b–12

[10b]Because <u>they did not receive</u>
    the love of the truth
    in order that they might be saved,
[11]and for this reason <u>God sends</u> them
    a working of deception
    in order that they might believe the lie,
[12]in order that all might be judged
    who did not believe the truth,
    but delighted in unrighteousness.

Many people find these verses to be extremely challenging. In verse 9, Paul says the lawless one operates "according to the working of Satan" (*energeian tou satana;* emphasis added). And then in 2 Thessalonians 2:11, he states very directly, "*God* sends them a working of deception [*energeian planēs*] in order that they might believe the lie" (emphasis added). The knee-jerk response to this passage is something like, How can a God of truth "send" deception? How can He, in the end time, act the same way Satan does? (Compare verse 11 with verse 9.)

In verses 9 and 11, Paul draws back the curtain and gives us a glimpse of the great controversy between Christ and Satan, which involves much more than just the affairs of this earth. Satan has accused

God of being unreasonable, of being a bully and a deceiver. In earth's final crisis, Satan's deception exposes the results of the decisions the wicked have already made (verse 12). In other words, the gospel brings out the worst in those whose hearts are set against God. Through the events of the end time, the minds and characters of Satan and his followers are clearly exposed to the judgment.

The process of delusion begins when people reject the gospel of Jesus Christ. Verse 10 says the wicked "did not receive the love of the truth in order that they might be saved." The offer of salvation is the subtext behind the apocalyptic powers of 2 Thessalonians 2. In the Middle Ages, the papacy, through its teachings and practices, undermined the gospel (verses 3, 4), and it will continue to do so until it is exposed by the events described in 2 Thessalonians 2:8–12. Thus, the final proclamation of the gospel (Matthew 24:14; Revelation 14:6, 7) sets the stage for both the final judgment and the delusions of the end time.

This means that in a sense, the two interpretations of verses 6 and 7 that we explored are both right. The interpretation that suggests the Roman Empire is the restrainer and power of restraint follows the pattern of Daniel 7 and Revelation 13 in identifying the historical face of apostasy. But throughout Christian history, it has been the gospel of Jesus Christ rather than political events that has functioned as the crucial line between good and evil. The antichrist is identified by its opposition to the gospel—the good news of the life, death, and heavenly reign of Jesus. And in the end, the timing of apocalyptic events is up to God and His plan of salvation. All the other actors in the drama play subordinate roles.

Two things in this passage relate directly to the identity of the restrainer. First, God is clearly in control of events on earth (2 Thessalonians 2:11)—in fact, He's so completely in control that He's said to have sent the working of Satan at the end. Second, it is also clear in this passage that the great deception of the end comes in the context of the widespread preaching of the gospel. Those who perish in the deception do so because "they did not receive the love of the truth in order that they might be saved" (verse 10).

And who is the restrainer? It would appear to be God Himself. Ultimately, only God can restrain Satan, and only God can hold back the Second Coming (Matthew 24:36). In the end, circumstances are such that God allows Satan to spring his last and greatest deception on a world that has deliberately rejected Christ.

The revelation of lawlessness is restrained in the sense that the gospel hasn't yet so clarified the issues that everyone on earth can make a settled and deliberate decision for or against Christ. It is the gospel that exposes Satan for who he really is. It is, therefore, the widespread and effective dissemination of the full gospel that precipitates Satan's strong reaction at the end. At that time, those who reject the gospel in its clarity will gladly receive the delusion.

Who then is the lawless one? In the ultimate and most personal sense, the lawless one could only be Satan himself. However, the parallels between the man of lawlessness of 2 Thessalonians 2:3, 4 and the little horn of Daniel (Daniel 8:9–12, 23–25; 11:31–39) remind us that Satan has always used the secular and religious authorities of this world to carry out his agenda of lawlessness. Through the centuries, both secular and religious Rome operated under the pretense of embodying the true worship of God, and in doing so, opposed the work of the gospel on earth. The counterfeits of the New Testament gospel fostered by this man of lawlessness were never fully unmasked to the public. But the day is coming when those who both preach and live the gospel will fully expose the enemy. He will be forced out of his comfortable anonymity—and he will, therefore, consider the end of this earth's history a time to take desperate measures (cf. Revelation 12:12).

Ellen G. White graphically describes Satan's great end-time deception in her powerful book *The Great Controversy:*

As the crowning act in the great drama of deception, Satan

147

himself will personate Christ. The church has long professed to look to the Saviour's advent as the consummation of her hopes. Now the great deceiver will make it appear that Christ has come. In different parts of the earth, Satan will manifest himself among men as a majestic being of dazzling brightness, resembling the description of the Son of God given by John in the Revelation. Revelation 1:13–15. . . .

Only those who have been diligent students of the Scriptures and *who have received the love of the truth* will be shielded from the *powerful delusion* that takes the world captive.[1]

What message did Paul want to communicate to the Thessalonians in chapter 2 of his second letter? Don't become alarmed, shaken, or deceived by messages that say the end is either imminent or already present (see 2 Thessalonians 2:1–3). Such messages are inappropriate until the gospel is known worldwide and the lawless one has been revealed (verses 3–12). The sobering part of all of this is that the lawless one will not be destroyed alone. All those whom he succeeds in deceiving will perish with him because they didn't "obey the gospel" (2 Thessalonians 1:8; cf. 2:10).

What counts as we approach the end is not how well we have calculated just when and how this revelation will come, but whether we have received and shared the love of the truth. The showdown may be worldwide, but the choice is still personal—it is yours and mine.

---

1. Ellen G. White, *The Great Controversy* (Mountain View, Calif.: Pacific Press®, 1950), 624, 625; emphasis added. A review of all of the comments Ellen G. White makes on 2 Thessalonians 2:1–12 revealed that she generally applies "the man of sin" and "the mystery of iniquity" to the long development and history of the papacy throughout the Christian era. Although she occasionally applies the concepts in 2 Thessalonians 2:4 to Satan, she regularly applies the "revelation of the lawless one" material in 2 Thessalonians 2:8–10 to Satan's "personation" of Christ just before the end.

Keeping the Church Faithful
(2 Thessalonians 2:13-3:18)

Churches are a lot like plants. As I pointed out in a previous chapter, if a plant doesn't grow, it will die. In other words, God designed plants to change. And what is true of plants is also true of churches. If they don't change, they also will die eventually.

But not all change is good. Change can lead us away from who we are. It can cause us to lose touch with God's purpose for us. While adapting to changing conditions is an important characteristic of healthy churches, they must never forget how God has led them in the past. Constructive change will always have an eye to "the traditions which you were taught" (2 Thessalonians 2:15). The best of these traditions reflects God's leading of the church in the past. Through revelation and Spirit-guided consensus, God has led the church to faithfulness. The light of the past helps the church navigate its way through the treacherous waters of change.

2 Thessalonians 2:13–17

¹³But <u>we are obligated</u>
    to give thanks to God always for you,
        brethren loved by God,
    because God chose you

from the beginning (as first fruits)
to salvation
in sanctification of the Spirit and
belief of the truth.
[14]With this end in view,
He called you
through our gospel,
so you might obtain the glory
of our Lord Jesus Christ.
[15]So then, brothers,
stand and hold fast the traditions which you were taught,
whether by word of mouth or
through our letter.
[16]May our Lord Jesus Christ Himself and
God our Father,
who loved us and
has given us
eternal encouragement and
dependable hope
by grace,
[17]comfort your hearts and
strengthen you
in every good deed and word.

The language of this section recalls the prayer at the beginning of 1 Thessalonians. It is almost as if Paul is intentionally returning to the place where he began, creating a natural conclusion to this pair of letters. Here he expresses his concern that the believers in Thessalonica not deviate from the path on which he has placed them.

Once again, the use of the words *brethren* and *brothers* (verses 13 and 15) signals a new turn in the letter, in this case the concluding turn. And once again Paul feels compelled to give thanks for the believers in Thessalonica (verse 13). Their lives provided evidence to Paul that they had been chosen unto salvation "as first fruits," or "from the beginning," depending on the Greek text one chooses to follow.*

To believe the truth, one must know the truth. That's why Paul is so concerned that the Thessalonians hold to the traditions they have been taught both by letters and by the spoken word (verse 15). People's grasp of truth often slips with the passage of time, so the church safeguards truth through both written and oral tradition. In the early days of the church, oral tradition was even preferred over written tradition. Oral tradition is less subject to unintentional distortion—gestures and tone of voice communicate meaning more accurately than words on a page do. That is why preaching as a method of communication never becomes outdated. However, written tradition, as in the letters of Paul, is less subject to intentional distortion by those who would alter the gospel for their own purposes. The Written Word provides a secure and unchangeable norm by which one can test the messages that come through preaching.

The second chapter ends with another wish prayer from Paul's pen (verses 16, 17). Paul prays that the Thessalonians might be strengthened by Jesus and His Father in "every good deed and word" (verse 17). The truth that has been worked into their lives will be shown through their words and actions. These changes are not primarily the results of the believer's attention and efforts; God provides strength and comfort "by grace," as a free gift (verse 16).

2 Thessalonians 3:1–5

¹Finally, brothers,
<u>pray</u> for us

---

* All of the manuscripts of this passage have the same letters; some manuscripts present the letters in question as a single word (*aparche,* "first fruits"); others have them divided into two words (*ap arche,* "from the beginning"). The earliest manuscripts of the New Testament didn't have punctuation or even spaces between the words, so either reading could be original. But the choice here doesn't affect the main point of the passage. While salvation is a gift according to the purpose of God, it is brought to the believer through sanctification by the Spirit and belief in the truth.

in order that the word of the Lord might progress
  and be glorified,
    just as it is with you,
²and in order that we might be delivered
  from out of place and evil men:
    for not all have faith.
³But faithful is the Lord,
  who will strengthen you
  and guard you against evil [or "the evil one"].
⁴And we have confidence in the Lord
    concerning you
  that what we command
    you are doing
    and will continue to do.
⁵Now may the Lord direct your hearts
    into the love of God and
    into the patient endurance of Christ.

The opening phrase of this passage ("Finally, brothers") signals that the reader is approaching the conclusion of the letter (cf. 2 Corinthians 13:11; Ephesians 6:10, and so on). As he did in 1 Thessalonians 5:25, Paul now asks for prayer regarding two spheres of his life. First, he wants the gospel to spread rapidly and to be honored through his work. His choice of words here in 2 Thessalonians 3:1 recalls the Olympic Games: first, the athletes run hard, and then they are honored. In a very gracious turn, Paul suggests that he would like to be as successful in evangelism as the Thessalonians have been!

Second, Paul wants them to pray that he will be delivered "from out of place and evil men" (verse 2). The expression here implies that he has in mind specific individuals whom the recipients of the letter would know.

Paul follows his prayer requests with a wordplay (verses 2, 3). Not all people have "faith" (trust in or commitment to God), but the Lord is "faithful" (dependable—One who inspires trust and commitment). The faithful Lord is dependable; the Thessalonians can trust Him to guard them against the evil one, or Satan. The good news is that while Satan is more powerful than we are, the Lord is more powerful than he is.

In today's world, many people laugh at the idea of personal evil in the form of a being called Satan. They think that both good and bad are simply the random consequences of cause and effect. But the Bible clearly asserts that Satan is real. In some parts of the world, it may be to his advantage to hide himself. But whenever the gospel is moving forward with power, he is forced to reveal himself, as Paul indicated in the middle of chapter 2. Ellen G. White says, "The thought that the righteousness of Christ is imputed to us, not because of any merit on our part, but as a free gift from God, is a precious thought. The enemy of God and man is not willing that this truth should be clearly presented; for he knows that if the people receive it fully, his power will be broken."[1] The greatest protection from the power of Satan is a full commitment to the gospel of Jesus Christ.

Paul ends this passage by once more commending the Thessalonians and offering another wish prayer on their behalf. He is confident that the Thessalonians are doing what he has asked and that they will continue to do so in spite of the opposition of Satan and the people he inspires. Paul prays that the Lord will direct the Thessalonians' attention to "the love of God" and "the patience of Christ" (verse 5). The goal of spiritual life is to be like God in love and like Christ in patient endurance.

2 Thessalonians 3:6–8

[6]Now <u>we command</u> you, brothers,
> in the name of our Lord Jesus Christ,
> <u>to keep away</u> from every brother

who walks in idleness [disorderly]
and not according to the tradition
which he received from us.
⁷For <u>you yourselves know</u>
how necessary it is to imitate us,
because we were not idle [disorderly] among you.
⁸Neither did we eat anyone's bread
without paying for it,
but in labor and hardship
we were working night and day
in order not to burden any of you.

In verse 4, Paul expressed confidence that the Thessalonians would obey whatever he commanded them. In verses 6–12, he puts them to the test. Appealing to the authority of Christ, Scripture, and his own teaching and example, he orders them to "keep away" (verse 6) from idle or disorderly members and to avoid associating with them (verse 14). Such a command can be quite challenging in a small community, but Paul was counting on their obedience.

Right from the beginning, obedience to Jesus' spoken words was mandatory for those who followed Him (Matthew 7:24–27; John 3:18–21). In the years after His ascension, His words and actions continued to be authoritative for the church (1 Thessalonians 4:15; Acts 20:35; 1 Corinthians 11:23–26). Then, through the inspiration of the Holy Spirit, the apostles were guided to interpret the words of Jesus and the significance of His actions correctly (John 15:26, 27; 16:13–15). And before the first generation of Christians had passed off the scene, the early church had concluded that the writings of the apostles were fully equal to those of the Old Testament prophets, so they could be called Scripture (2 Peter 3:2, 16). In 2 Thessalonians 3, Paul explicitly claims authority for his letters—in effect, he was claiming that they are as authoritative as the Old Testament (verses 6, 14).

In New Testament times, *tradition* wasn't a dirty word; it represented the church's memory of the sayings and actions of Jesus and included the oral teachings and the writings of the apostles. Tradition, as the early Christians understood it, functioned in much the same way as do the Scriptures for us today. It included commands that were to be obeyed.

For the Thessalonians, tradition meant more than just Paul's letters. All that he'd said to them while he was in Thessalonica was included, and so were his actions, which they were to imitate. The fact that Paul worked hard to support himself in Thessalonica not only showed that he cared for them (1 Thessalonians 2:9), but it also formed a tradition that he expected them to apply to their own lives. Paul wasn't idle while he was among them. He didn't eat other people's food without paying for it. He labored night and day so as not to be a burden to anyone—and he intended the Thessalonian believers to be self-sufficient too. Any member of the church there who lived differently was "out of order." (More on that later.)

2 Thessalonians 3:9–12

⁹It is not because we have no authority,
    but in order that we might give you an example,
      so you could imitate us.
¹⁰For even when we were with you,
we constantly commanded you like this:
    "If anyone does not wish to work,
      neither should he eat."
¹¹For we hear
    that some among you are walking in idleness [disorderly],
      instead of being busy,
      they are busybodies.
¹²We command and urge such people
    in the Lord Jesus Christ
    that *working* in quietness,
      each might eat his own bread.

The Greek language has more than one word that can be translated as "but." In 2 Thessalonians 3:8, 9, Paul uses, twice, the very strongest "but" to introduce an extreme contrast. Paul and the apostles didn't freeload, *but* instead, they worked night and day (verse 8). They didn't work because of weakness; they deliberately worked for their living to set an example for the believers. Paul must have sensed right from the start that there would be unique challenges in this particular community.

What else can we learn about the nature of the challenges the church in Thessalonica posed?

A significant number of the members there were idle—disorderly, or out of order (verses 6, 7, 11). The key word in the original language is *ataktos,* which is based on the root word *taktos.* The core meaning of *taktos* is to arrange, to put things in order, or to give orders, whether in business, government, or military matters. In Greek, putting the letter alpha in front of a word turns that word into its opposite, much as we do in English with the prefixes *un-* (clear/unclear) and *dis-* (regard/disregard). So, when *a* is added to *taktos,* the resulting word, *ataktos,* means "disorderly."

The Jewish philosopher Philo used *ataktos* to describe the condition of the world before Creation (Genesis 1:2), and the Jewish historian Josephus used it of the disorder seen in a defeated army. The word was also used of uncontrolled crowds milling about in a disorderly fashion. The *ataktos* person is someone who evades obligations, who sets himself or herself outside the societal order. Since a garden tends to fall into a disorderly condition without significant human effort by weeding, trimming, and cultivating, the word can have the extended meaning of idleness: an *ataktos* person is someone who should be working but isn't.

But *ataktos* is not a synonym for laziness. The real issue with *ataktos* people isn't that they have little motivation to work; it's more a matter of them having an irresponsible attitude. The disorderly members in Thessalonica weren't just sitting around; they were going from place to place creating disruptions. They spent their time discussing theology or criticizing the behavior of others instead of earning their keep. In 2 Thessalonians 3:11, Paul uses a wordplay that could be literally translated as "instead of working, they're working around." They were minding everyone's business but their own. So, although *ataktos* is often translated as "idleness" (e.g., see 1 Thessalonians 5:14; 2 Thessalonians 3:6, 7, 11, NIV), it has more to do with a disruptive attitude than simple laziness. That Paul had to address this so often (see also 1 Thessalonians 4:9–12) indicates it was a major problem for the church in Thessalonica.

The rioting mentioned in Acts 17:5–8 was based, first of all, on malicious accusations from Jews who felt their position in the city was threatened by the arrival of the Christians—particularly in light of the recent (A.D. 49) expulsion of Jews from Rome. But as we saw earlier, there was also a misunderstanding based on expectations aroused by the Cabirus cult (see chapter 3 of this book). The language Paul used in his letters to the Thessalonians, however, suggests that some of the blame for the rioting belonged to the new believers themselves. They brought a disruptive attitude with them into the church, and that attitude soon caused trouble, not only in the church, but also in the wider society.

As an apostle, Paul could have required the church to provide him with housing, food, and money, but Paul worked "night and day" so as not to burden them (1 Thessalonians 2:9). If Paul's example were the only thing that called them to work hard, some could have claimed that the tradition wasn't clear. But Paul had also addressed this issue with words. During the short time he was with them in person, he often said, "If anyone does not wish to work, neither should he eat" (2 Thessalonians 3:10). Paul didn't invent this saying; it is widely attested in the ancient world, in both Jewish and Greek documents. This is the other side of the coin when it comes to helping the poor; sometimes it is wiser to withdraw support than to offer more of it.

In some ways, following Paul's counsel is even more challenging now than it was in the ancient world. Today, increasing numbers of people work in service industries, where they spend their lives teaching, healing, ministering, and directing rather than working with their hands. In our world, machines are doing more and more of the hard labor.

Paul's counsel may be particularly apropos to the typical office today. In the absence of hard manual labor, people thrown together in an office, even a church office, can easily fall into the same trap as the idle Thessalonian believers did. They can spend their time talking about theology, the personality quirks of others, or the perceived slights that people working closely together always experience. The result is a toxic atmosphere of criticism and blame—which sounds a lot like what was going on in the church at Thessalonica.

Paul's advice? Mind your own business. Keep your focus on the Lord. Don't become weary doing good for others. Do your work "in quietness" (2 Thessalonians 3:12; see also 1 Thessalonians 4:11), managing your own affairs. Determine to make a difference that's more positive than negative. Follow the loving, forgiving, merciful example of Jesus and the apostles. And if all else fails, obey the commandment because God said you should!

2 Thessalonians 3:13–15

[13]As for you, brothers,
<u>do not become weary</u> in doing good.
   [14]If anyone does not obey our word
      through this letter,
<u>take notice</u> of him.
<u>Do not associate</u> with him,
   in order that he might become ashamed.
[15]And <u>do not regard</u> him as an enemy,
but <u>admonish him</u> like a brother.

Keeping the Church Faithful (2 Thessalonians 2:13-3:18)

Church discipline is one of the most difficult issues congregations face. Every errant member is another member's brother, mother, son, cousin, or best friend. Some members prefer never to discipline anyone, and others prefer harsh sanctions. How does a church find the will of God in the midst of competing interests?

Matthew 18:15–20 suggests a clear and simple process. First, start with a one-on-one conversation between the offender and the one most offended. The context indicates that wherever possible, forgiveness is to be the goal of that conversation (verses 21–35). Second, if the first step doesn't go well, to avoid confusion as to what is said by whom, the offended member is to take one or two other people along. Only after these first two steps have been followed should the matter go to the church in a business session. Then, if the offender doesn't respond to the church as a whole, he or she is to be treated as "a Gentile and a tax collector" (Matthew 18:17, ESV).

But there's a conundrum in Jesus' instruction. What does it mean to treat someone as one would treat a Gentile and a tax collector? There are at least two possibilities, and they're very different. On the one hand, Jesus could be calling the church to shun the offender the way the Jews shunned Gentiles and tax collectors. But on the other hand, He could be calling them to treat the offender the way *He* treated Gentiles and tax collectors—with compassion and forgiveness!

Applying Matthew 18 and 2 Thessalonians 3 in contemporary life is a challenge. No two people are alike. No two situations are alike. In some cases, forgiveness softens the heart of an offender and brings reconciliation to the church. In other cases, the offender may respond only to a love that is tough enough to confront and administer consequences. This is why the General Conference doesn't disfellowship anyone—such delicate processes are best handled by the local church, where the offender is known best.

The effectiveness of tough love isn't a license for abuse. According to 2 Thessalonians 3:15, the person being shunned is still to be treated like family. Discipline is not personal; it is a public act, done for the good of the whole community. The church withdraws by publicly exposing the problem. But while it isn't appropriate for the church and the offender to have a buddy-buddy relationship, believers are to remain courteous toward that person. Those who discipline must remain aware that the offender is a brother "for whom Christ died" (Romans 14:15, NKJV; 1 Corinthians 8:11, NKJV).

2 Thessalonians 3:16–18

[16]Now <u>may the very Lord of peace give you peace</u>
    at all times
    in every way.
<u>The Lord be</u> with you all.
[17]The greeting in my own hand: Paul.
<u>This is</u> a sign in every letter.
<u>This is</u> how I write.
[18]The <u>grace</u> of our Lord Jesus Christ <u>be</u> with you all.
Amen.

In verse 16, Paul uses three *p*'s to emphasize the importance of the gift of peace he wishes the Thessalonian believers to have: *pantos,* "all times"; *panti,* "every way"; *panton,* "you all." The church has suffered persecution from without and disruption from within. What the members need most is peace, and Jesus Christ, the Lord of peace, is the best Source of that peace.

I believe Paul would also wish that all who have read this book about his letters to the Thessalonians might have peace too.

---

1. Ellen G. White, *Gospel Workers* (Washington, D.C.: Review and Herald®, 1948), 161.